Law, Technology and Women:
Challenges and Opportunities

Law, Technology and Women:

Challenges and Opportunities

STELLINA JOLLY
Asst. Prof., LLM, Ph.D.

Reference Press
4831/24, Ansari Road, Darya Ganj,
New Delhi-110002
Tel. : 23260807, 41563444
Fax : 011-41563334
E-mail: info@essessreference.com
www.essessreference.com

REFERENCE PRESS
4831/24, Ansari Road,
Darya Ganj,
New Delhi-110 002.

Tel.: 23260807, 41563444
Fax: 41563334
E-mail: info@essessreference.com
www.essessreference.com

Rs.625/-

First Published - 2010

ISBN: 978-81-8405-058-5

Published By Reference Press and printed at Salasar Imaging Systems

PRINTED IN INDIA

Contents

Introduction

"All rights are universal, indivisible and interdependent and interrelated."

The accelerated progress of science and technology is indisputable, as is its impact on economic, social, and cultural aspects. New discoveries in genetics, pharmacology, and assisted reproductive technologies will soon allow us to modify ourselves and our children in ways never before possible Technological developments raise a variety of ethical and legal questions that compel us to reexamine our traditional morals and how they now apply to novel circumstances. With these advances come profound questions about what it means to be human and what kind of future world we want to live in. Ethical and legal issues surrounding the various scientific and technological developments can no longer be dismissed as the stuff of science fiction. Debate about these questions is under way in academia, in the political arena, and within religious communities. Policy makers are addressing ethical questions when they consider whether to fund stem-cell research. Courts are facing ethics questions when they consider which of three "parents" — an egg donor, a gestational mother, and a social mother — should receive custody of a child. The media cover these issues with high emotion.

An analyses of the human right charters, reveals that initially there was no direct and explicit emphasis given to the scientific and technological aspects in relation to human right. Some of the challenges and difficulties raised by the technological breakthrough are covered very generally at the international level by the Universal Declaration on Human Rights (UDHR) the International Covenant on Civil and Political Rights (ICCPR), and the International Covenant on Economic, Social and Cultural Rights (ICESCR). Specifically United Nations woke up to the threat faced by the humanity in wake of technological growth with the declaration on the Use of Scientific and Technological Progress in the Interests of Peace and for the Benefit of Mankind, promulgated in 1975, United Nations later elaborated and backed it up with a catena of declaration including the Declaration on Human Genome and Human Rights, Bioethics and Human Rights etc.

Turning our attention to India, ours is one of the few jurisdictions which have grafted various fundamental rights as part of constitution. Besides these several statutes are enacted to protect and promote human rights catering different communities, groups and areas. Judiciary has also equally championed the cause of Human Rights. But it is to be regretfully noted that in our effort to check the negative impact of science and technology on society we have fallen behind various jurisdictions who have drafted specific initiatives into their legal framework.

In spite of women's important contribution to the scientific and technological progress, the International and national programs and policies for human right have not fully addressed gender equity as a fundamental component for achieving the goals It is to be noted that despite the clamor in nearly every where regarding the threat of science and technology on various aspects of human dignity, women's voices are under-represented. Hinsch notes, "Without a voice in shaping the legislation and policies that affect their lives, women will have to contest potentially dire consequences after the fact. We must be vigilant about creating policies that are thoughtfully drafted by-and for-all people."

This book tries to analyze how far gender concerns find its place in National and international Human Right doctrines.

It deals with some of the contentious issues of science and technology with its impact on women. Focus of the book ranges from Impact of Human Genome Project on women dignity and rights. Reproductive Rights, Surrogacy Issues, Stem cell research and question of women's health etc Although the book does not claim to be exhaustive, it shows to what extent the specificity of issues related to women in relation to scientific and technological issues has sometimes been underestimated in Legal and Human Right framework.

Chapter 1: International Human Right Regime and Gender Concerns

Human Rights is as old as the human civilization, But the establishment of United Nations saw the beginning of the modern era of human rights. Since its emergence in 1945, the United Nations (UN) has been one of the key international actors in the field of human rights. The Concept of Human Right has undergone tremendous transformation over the years to encompass variety of rights like that of children's and women's. With Regard to gender rights U.N has played a significant role championing women's human rights and promoting equality between the sexes through conventions and declarations. These laws have played a positive role in uplifting the rights of women however these measures suffer from certain drawbacks and it can be argued that this partly explains the persistence of the problem and underdevelopment of women. The first chapter describes the evolution of international human rights relevant to women's rights and shows how specific universal and regional international instruments can provide a framework for understanding the nature of State obligations to protect women's rights. This chapter brings out the structure of international human right regime, including Universal declaration on Human Rights 1948, International Covenant on Civil and Political Rights 1966, International Covenant on Economic, Social and Cultural Rights 196. Chapter will give special emphasis to the efforts taken by the United Nations to tackle the threat to women's dignity and rights in wake of the developments in Science and Technology including Declaration on Human Genome and Human Rights and Declaration on Bio- Ethics. The purpose of this chapter. is to examine the efficacy of the legal frame work for promoting and protecting women's rights, the chapter explores the strengths and weaknesses of the international Human Right laws to protect the rights of women in the wake of new scientific and biotechnological improvements.

Chapter 2 : Human Genome Project and Genetic Testing: Safeguarding Gender Genetic Privacy

Human Genome Project (HGP) is an effort to produce a detailed genetic and physical map of all human chromosomes. The complete sequencing of the human genetic code offers numerous opportunities for scientific progress and advancements in medicine. However, genetics has become not only a vast scientific enterprise, but legal and ethical issue as well. Because of their central role in reproduction women are likely to be affected differently, and more significantly, by the information the HGP and possible genetic test generates. It is important to identify inequities that may emerge from gender differences and to consider ways in which they may be avoided, reduced, or overcome. This chapter describes the potential impact of the "new genetics" on women. This chapter specially deals with the issue of gender privacy in genetic testing. Much has been written on the right of employers and insurers to gain access to the results of genetic testing; this chapter focuses on an area that has received less attention in the current discourse—whether or not family members are entitled to know the results of an individual's genetic testing even over the individual's objection. The author notes that in most discussions of such family entitlement, gender differences are ignored, The author feels that given the power of various health-related issue to influence the incidence of domestic violence, torture discrimination, and alter existing family relationships for women it is in women's best interests to adopt a conservative, perhaps absolutist, requirement of privacy.

Chapter 3: Stem Cell Research, Impact on Health and Dignity of Women: A Legal and Ethical analysis

"Which comes first—the egg or the cure?" asks an advertisement alluring young women to supply their eggs for stem cell research. The propaganda around stem cell research and the ensuing media concentration have raised public hopes that research will soon lead to cures for chronic diseases such as diabetes and Parkinson's. These hopes overshadow serious risks associated with one approach to stem cell research that has been receiving increased attention from scientists. This technique, somatic cell nuclear transfer (SCNT) or "research cloning", raises serious concerns because it requires a huge number of women's eggs and poses a host of problems for women's health and dignity. These problems include the short-term health risks associated with the egg extraction process, a lack of information about long-term effects, the potential for exploitation of economically vulnerable women, and the possibility of increased co modification of women's bodies. The Chapter critically analyzes the ethical and legal issues rising out of Stem cell research in relation to women rights .Chapter explore the Legislative and judicial response in this field with special reference to India,

Chapter 4: Reproductive Rights: Promoting Self Determination of Women

Sexual and reproductive self-determination of women was recognized as a human right through the various U.N Conferences in Vienna, Cairo, Copenhagen and Beijing. But in developing countries, reproductive self-determination is a goal still unfulfilled. Acute poverty, religious fundamentalism, lack of health and Nutrition, and women's subordination in the family and in society, adversely affects women's reproductive self-determination. The ability to make choices in their reproductive lives will have significant implications that go far beyond individuals to society as a whole. The Chapter brings out the substantive and procedural Legal frame work in relation to Reproductive rights of women including right of abortion. The purpose of the chapter is to analyze the efficacy and limitation of Reproductive rights in improving the status and dignity of women. The chapter explores the strengths and weaknesses of the policy measures aimed at controlling reproductive rights and makes appropriate recommendations for its improvement.

Chapter 5 : Renting a Womb: Technology and Surrogacy Rights

The arrival of new scientific reproductive technologies has conjured up fresh and apparently obstinate debates about bioethics and current values in the field of family law. Surrogacy, unquestionably, is the most contentious of them all. Recently India became the first country to legalize Surrogacy. It was in done in wake of the increasing instances of commercial surrogacy fuelled by a booming medical tourism assisted by low medical costs and a status-conscious middle class seeking to fulfill its financial needs. This chapter examines the changing social and political meaning of surrogacy over the years since this issue first attracted public attention in the context of the Baby M case in the 1980s.Chapter will critically evaluate the Assisted Reproductive bill introduced in the parliament. This chapter supports the legitimization of surrogacy from the standpoint of affirmative fundamental right of life guaranteed under Article 21 of the Constitution of India and the liberties guaranteed under the Constitution but with adequate legal safeguard against women's exploitation.

Chapter 6 : Climate Change and Impact on Women: Need for a New Legal Paradigm

Climate Change is one of the most important global environmental challenges, with implications for food production, water supply, health, energy, etc. Although the hazards associated with Climate Change impact societies all over the world, it is important to recognize that they have a different effect on men and women, ethnic groups, social classes, age groups, etc. Despite the importance of recognizing gender-related differences, both the United Nations Framework Convention on Climate Change and Kyoto Protocol fail to recognize this. The Chapter discusses the impact of Climate Change with special reference to women. Chapter further looks at the possibilities and limitations of the role of women in mitigating Climate Change. The chapter critically analyzes the various legislative and policy options initiated to combat Climate change and will analyze whether gender concerns finds a place in it. Chapter strongly brings out a case for making climate change discourse more gender sensitive.

Chapter 7 : Information and Communication Technology and Pornography: A Threat to the Dignity of Women

In recent years the information and communication technology has proliferated the world. Although these technologies have brought great development across the globe one can not completely say that it has all been a success but it has also to a great extent brought some reparations. Amazingly, many people do not seem to see the negative effects these fast developing technologies have brought to countries and people. Information and communication Technology has precipitates the spread of crime such as internet sex terrorism, prostitution, child trafficking, identity theft, pornography etc. The purpose of this chapter is to argue for the need for systematic information systems research within the field of digital women pornography. "The Chapter analyses the impact of new Information and Communication Technology (ICT) revolution on Pornography. Chapter discusses the impact of pornography on women and critically analyses the international and national legal response in this regard. This chapter provides an overview and discussion of key issues, dilemmas and challenges. It points to possible modifications and at ways to devise new dimensions to pornography regulations.

1
International Human Right Regime and Gender Concerns

The world of civilization is made of male and female. Ideally each should complement each other and dependant on each other. If one is defective, the other will necessarily be incomplete, and perfection cannot be attained. Just as physical accomplishment is only complete with two haves, so man and woman, the two parts of the social body, must be perfect. It is not natural that either should remain undeveloped, and until both are perfected the happiness of the human world will not be realized.[1]

But the actual reality is far from this idealistic state. One part of humanity, women are exposed to a continuum of violence from the time of conception to death. It assumes various forms from female foeticide taking place in the womb, domestic violence taking place in the home, where the woman or girl usually knows the assailant; to outside the home where females are exposed to arbitrary violence by people employing them, to the large-scale systematic mass violence against women found in war like situations. All these types of violence directed against women can be ascribed to a single cause - the patriaral mind of society and lack of women's voice in the decision making process and the social tolerance of human rights abuses against women.[2] This chapter brings out the structure of international women's Human right regime including 1979 Convention against all forms of Discrimination, Vienna Conference on Human Rights, Millennium development goals, Declaration on Bio ethics and human rights and procedures of these institutions. The purpose of this chapter is to examine the efficacy of the legal frame work in promoting women's human rights. The chapter explores the strengths and weaknesses of the international laws on women's rights and makes appropriate recommendations for its improvement especially in wake of scientific and technological development.

International Human Rights Law: Product of Second World War

International law believed to be the product of Christian civilization traditionally coordinated and controlled inter-state relationships. To begin with states were the only entities with complete international personality.[3] The subject matter of the international legal system has continued to grow and today it is at its most expansive stage including Individuals and Organizations. Various atrocities inflicted on individuals by successive governments gradually brought Individuals to the forefront of international law. With the growing importance of individuals under international law the scope and ambit of international law expanded to include Human Rights.

It is believed that human rights originated with the birth of man.[4] But Human Right as known today is believed to have come into existence much later. The first collective expression of Human right was in the form of the famous documents of rights the Magna Carta of 1215 AD of England,[5] Later the American Bill of Rights of 1791,[6] The French Declaration of the Rights of man of 1792,[7] resulted in establishing and bringing Human Rights to the fore front of international and municipal law. The first truly international human rights instrument was the 1926 Slavery convention.[8] The current human rights system emerged after the creation of the United Nations (UN) after World War.[9] The barbaric treatment of peoples during the war, in particular under fascist regimes, shocked the world into establishing an international legal order to regulate and try to prohibit human rights abuses by the state.

An analysis of U.N charter clearly depicts the concern makers of the charter had for the promotion and protection of human rights. Article 1 of the UN charter declares promotion of human right as one of its main goals. The major goals of U.N consists of

- the *maintenance of international peace and security* by means of peaceful conflict settlement and collective measures against threats;
- the *creation of friendly relations among nations* based on the principle of self-determination of peoples;
- *international cooperation to resolve problems* of economic, social, cultural and humanitarian character and to
- *Promote respect for human rights* and fundamental freedoms.[10]

In order to fulfill its tasks of promoting Human Right, Economic and Social security Council (ECOSOC) has established a range of subsidiary bodies, including the Commission on Human Rights (CHR) and the Commission on the Status of Women (CSW).[11] Its basic functions were to prepare recommendations for the ECOSOC on promoting women's rights and on urgent problems requiring immediate action in the field of women's rights.[12] Initially the CSW focused on fact-finding activities to elucidate the scope of sex-based discrimination. A global survey on the status of women's rights conducted by the CSW in 1947 revealed that of 74 sovereign states 25 had not granted full political rights to their female citizens, including the right to vote or hold public office.[13]

Regarding the scope and ambit of Human Right treaties enunciated and initiated by U.N, initially securing legal equality occupied the first priority; The international system started with the Universal Declaration on Human Rights in 1948[14] and has been further developed ever since, consisting of various independent rights including right against torture, discrimination etc as the large number of specialized human rights treaties shows. The underlying reason for this sort of approach is that the modem human right system was created by white, educated, propertied men. They devised a system which revolved around their fears - losing civil and political rights and identity. But with time the promotional dimension of the regime has gotten stronger, as human rights norms formed an "interdependent and synergistically interactive system of guarantees." [15] However, what *is* universal and consistent in practice is the persistent disregard for the safeguarding of human rights of women. Following the laissez-faire principle women were considered to be equal to men and it was presumed that the existing human right structure which more or less cater to a wide range of male concerns would adequately cover female needs too. The international structure of the human rights regime is built on the stillness and exclusion of women. Further despite the significant advances made in increasing the scope of Human rights, the structure of the system has remained largely unchanged. Human rights have, unfortunately, been subject to an artificial division into originally first and second generation and more recently third generation rights.[16]

The first generation of human rights, the civil and political rights, emerged with the French and US-American revolutions over 200 years ago. The core construction of this generation of rights is the freedom of expression for autonomous citizens and their protection from governmental arbitrary action such as detention or torture. The second generation of human rights spells out the social, economic and cultural rights dispensable for a life lived in dignity. Third-generation human rights are those rights that go beyond the mere civil and social, as expressed in many progressive documents of international law, including right to self determination and environment. It should also acknowledged that womens rights falls into all generation of rights though many experts believe that More than the first generation, second and third generation of human rights explains the rights of women better as it includes the situation of women in principle, since it deals with the rights that "affect, define and limit the lives of women".[17]

The basis of present women's human right structure lies in the establishment of U.N. At the time of its establishment in 1945, the United Nations was the first global organization that unambiguously and unequivocally included the encouragement and endorsement of human rights, including the human rights of women, in its agenda of action. In the times to follow, this directive got converted into an unparalleled framework for the emancipation and empowerment of millions of women worldwide.

In the history of women's rights four period can be identified First phase comprising the period from 1945 to 1962 was of " ensuring the legal foundations of equality" What is noteworthy is that this attempt at securing legal equality occurred in a time of very little consciousness regarding the lower position of women in the political economic and social ladder. The UN vehemently addressed the legal and factual barriers women were confronted with. Second, the role of women in development was recognized which was mainly between 1963 to 1975. In this phase, "the focus broadened from codification of equality of rights under the law to encompass the economic and social realities of women's daily lives." [18] In the subsequent period which was United Nations Decade for Women (1976-1985), the international community's understanding of women became profoundly transformed: they were no longer seen as a particular group that had to be treated separately, but as essential contributors to each society's development process. [19]The fourth period (1986-1996) was shaped by the attempt to implement the visions formulated during the UN Decade for Women, for example the mainstreaming of gender equality into all activities of the UN, and by developing increasingly complex standards for the achievement of gender equality. The fifth period is shaped by a new threat to women's rights .The progress taking place in various fields of Science and technology and consequent threat on their dignity.

Securing the Legal Foundations of Equality

In the early stages of the United Nations' subsistence, there was not much consciousness and information on women's low status. It is evidenced in the first General Assembly meeting of the United Nations in 1946, only a handful of women participated as official delegates. U.N slowly build up the awareness of women's rights. In fact the main achievements of the U.N at this stage were consciousness-raising and standard- setting concerning basic legal rights for women The only formal place where womens rights issue could be articulated properly was the Commission on the Status of Women (CSW). Commission on the Status of Women influenced the drafting processes of various core documents, in particular the UN Charter and the Universal Declaration of Human Rights.[20] At the time of the drafting of the Universal Declaration on Human Rights (UDHR), CSW, pushed for integrating a gender perspective.

Universal Declaration on Human Rights (UDHR)

The UDHR is accepted worldwide as customary international law that binds all countries. If you analyze the application of this declaration specifically to the progress in terms of gender. The gender-sensitivity of the Declaration finds its expression in three ways: first, it contains some, direct references to women's rights. Article 16 talks on the equal rights of men and women "as to marriage, during marriage and at its dissolution" It underscores the "free and full consent" of both intending spouses to get married. [21] Article 25 states Everyone has the right to a standard of living adequate for the health and well-being of himself and of his family, including food, clothing, housing and medical care and necessary social services, and the right to security in the event of unemployment, sickness, disability, widowhood, old age or other lack of livelihood in circumstances beyond his control. Further Clause (2) declares that motherhood and childhood are entitled to special care and assistance. All children, whether born in or out of wedlock, shall enjoy the same social protection.[22]

Second, in almost the entire document, gender-neutral terms such as "everyone" and "no one" are used. For instance preamble reads "whereas the peoples of the United Nations have in the Charter reaffirmed their faith in fundamental human rights, in the dignity and worth of the human person and in the equal rights of men and women and have determined to promote social progress and better standards of life in larger freedom, [23] Further the wording of article 1 is in gender neutral terms - "*All men* are born free and equal in dignity and rights ...and should act towards one another *like brothers*," was changed into "All human beings" This applies to article 21 clause (3), on "free and equal suffrage" and to article 23 (2), conferring the right to equal pay for equal work to "everyone, without any discrimination."[24]

United Nations did not stop with a mere declaration of rights. It embarked on converting these principles into reality. The Convention on the Political Rights of Women, which was adopted by the General Assembly in 1952 actually reiterated the spirit of the Universal Declaration,[25] The convention proclaimed the right of women to hold public office and exercise all public functions established by national law" [26] The Convention on Consent to Marriage, Minimum Age of Marriage and Registration of Marriages was adopted in 1962 aimed at freedom and autonomy of parties. [27] This first period was successful in international consciousness raising and standard setting,

Recognition of Role of Women in Development

Once the Universal Declaration of Human Rights was adopted, the Commission on Human Rights, main body to promote human rights set out to translate its principles into international treaties that protected specific rights. Given the too wide and expanded nature of the rights, the General Assembly decided to draft two Covenants codifying political, economic and social rights envisaged in the Universal Declaration. They reached a consensus on the form and modalities of the covenants in 1966, and the United Nations General Assembly adopted the International Covenant on Economic, Social and Cultural Rights[28] and the International Covenant on Civil and Political Rights that year.[29]

International Covenant on Economic, Social and Cultural Rights (ICESCR)

The ICESCR sets out elaborately a variety of social and economic rights. The relevant provisions to the discussion are Art 3 which obliges the state parties to the present covenant. to ensure the equal right of men and women to the enjoyment of all civil and political rights set forth in the present Covenant [30] Further Art 7(1) guarantees Fair wages It reads "Fair wages and equal remuneration for work of equal value without distinction of any kind, in particular women being guaranteed conditions of work not inferior to those enjoyed by men, with equal pay for equal work;" [31] Convention also envisage special protection measure for mothers" Special protection is to be accorded to mothers during a reasonable period before and after childbirth. During such period working mothers should be accorded paid leave or leave with adequate social security benefits. "[32] Further on similar terms with UDHR all the rights guaranteed under the covenant are gender neutral and are meant to be applied too all men and women equally. For instance preamble proclaims that Women and men are entitled to economic, social, and cultural rights that allow them dignity and freedom as individuals Art 2(2) guarentees equality of treatment " No human being should be treated differently or have their rights denied because of their sex, race, color, language, religion, political, opinion, national or social origin, property, birth, or other status. [33]

International Covenant on Civil and Political Rights (ICCPR)

The ICCPR provides some account of the civil and political rights held by individuals in relation to the States. Relevant article to the discussion are Art 3 emphasize the Parties to undertake measures to ensure the equal right of men and women to the enjoyment of all civil and political rights set forth in the Covenant. Art 7 declares "Sentence of death shall not be imposed for crimes committed by persons below eighteen years of age and shall not be carried out on pregnant women.[34] Covenant recognizes the right of men and women of marriageable age to marry and to found a family and further clarifies that. No marriage shall be entered into without the free and full consent of the intending spouses. [35] Some of the rights which can be so read to include women's rights. Women have the right to be treated equally under the law and to be protected by the law without discrimination. [36] No human being should be treated differently or have their rights denied because of their sex, race, color, language, religion, political, opinion, national or social origin, property, birth, or other status. [37] Women have the right to freedom of thought, conscience, and religion Women have the right to freely express their opinion without fear or punishment.[38] The major positive element of this convention can be gathered from the fact that States are obliged to take legislative or administrative measures to give effect to the rights set out in the ICCPR. [39] Moreover if a country has ratified the ICCPR Optional Protocol, its individual citizens can lodge complaints of transgressions before the Human Rights Committee set up under the convention.[40]

Despite the improvement and progress made in codifying women's rights in law, "it became clear during the 1960s that the legal status and securing substantial and procedural equality of women was only one aspect of a larger theme, the ultimate aim has to be the advancement of women in complete social and economic context." [41] The initiative was taken by CSW which started to discuss ways to grant women equal access to education, employment opportunities and health care, and analyzed the specific needs of women in community and rural development, agricultural, and family planning. These discussion and studies aimed at exploring the possibilities of women in socio-economic development led to the certain positive results. The concept of development achieved a new meaning. The areas and issues which were considered to be unrelated to development were made part of the study of development. For Instance the first Conference on Human Rights, held in Teheran 1968, mentioned family planning for the first time as a basic human right, Shortly after the Teheran conference the ECOSOC requested a report on the interrelation of the status of women and family planning, which was finalized in 1973.[42] It concluded that "family planning offers obvious benefits to women as individuals, especially with regard to their health, education or employment and their roles in family. The second phase of the UN's engagement to improve the status of women was more comprehensive than the first one: the debate went beyond women's legal equality and recognized their disadvantaged socio-economic position Women's Rights are Human rights.

The idea of women right being Human Right was fresh, new and revolting, Specially because theoretically women have generally never been denied the fundamental human rights. In 1945, the UN Charter followed by Bill of Rights afforded to women and men equal economic, social, cultural, political and civil rights. But since women occupied low position in the social ladder the benefits of these rights never percolated to them and abuses and violations of the established human right continued unabated and often got ignored. [43] If you take the any possible scenario of human right violations, women, are the worst sufferers be it in a war or conflict or even new developments threatening human rights. Their numbers comes in prominence among the list of world's refugees and poverty stricken people. But since human right regime never took into account seriously the rights of women constant prejudice against their rights became part of established systems.[44]

To declare and accept women's rights as human rights feminist movements played a positive role. They emphasized the fact that a right based regime can not marginalize any group. In the face of marginalization and oppression of any group of people the concept of human right fails and looses its significance. Collective and Universal human rights cannot be a facade for oppressive institutions. The protection of human rights is the birth right of everyone.

Following an active support and effort by feminists the year 1975 was declared International Women's Year by the United Nations and proclaimed certain goals which are to be achieved by year 2000. Progress in meeting these goals were subject to evaluation at five year intervals.[45] The decade saw much progress and movements with regard to women's protection rights. The decade concentrated on development of women and recognized the contribution of women in development strategy .They also acknowledged that without the positive contribution of female's real development can not be achieved.

The three international women's conferences were initiated as part of the Decade – Mexico in 1975, Copenhagen in 1980, and Nairobi in 1985 – These conferences became the global platforms for dialogue and for the discussion on concrete measures. In Mexico, delegations adopted the World Plan of Action that contained actions to be taken to promote the advancement of women for the next decade.[46]

Another notable achievement of the decade was the focus on discrimination Deviating from the earlier human right approaches which focused on securing equality the conferences stressed on ending all discrimination against women. It is to be emphasized that Discrimination on the basis of sex is explicitly named as a violation of human rights in all the basic human rights documents including UN Charter, and Bill of Rights. From a legalistic perspective women's rights were always considered to be Human rights. But the ground realities were clearly different and this was sought to be changed by feminist movement and the successive women's conferences. [47] One of the most notable achievements of the Decade for Women was the Convention on the Elimination of All Forms of Discrimination Against Women (CEDAW). [48]

CEDAW: Declaration on Women's Rights

The CEDAW Convention can be seen as the outcome of a long process to bring the concerns of women into the human rights framework. It has often been called as the declaration on women's rights equating with Universal declaration of Rights It is in fact hailed as a milestone for the rights of women due to its unprecedented comprehensiveness and legally binding character. The CEDAW Convention was adopted by the General Assembly in 1979 and entered into force in 1981.

The process of creating the CEDAW Convention developed in various stages. The CSW started working on the draft at its 1965 meeting in Teheran based on the suggestions and comments of 33 governments, Secondly from 1977 to 1979 three Working Groups of the Third Committee to the

General Assembly continued the drafting process. Third, in a few sessions in December 1979, the Third Committee as a whole came to a final agreement that was followed by immediate adoption in the General Assembly the international operationalization of CEDAW consists of the CEDAW Committee as monitoring body and its international support structures.

The Preamble enumerates the existing international human rights instruments relevant for the status of women and expresses the need to go beyond them, since discrimination against women continues to exist. It underlines the crucial contribution of women to the wellbeing of family and society that is not fully recognized, and calls for a change in the traditional role models for men and women Convention aimed to rectify the inferior status of women in society. The Women's Convention is an amalgam of equality principles and anti-discrimination ethic. The purpose of Article 1 is not merely to attain gender neutrality, but to articulate the elimination of *all* forms of discrimination against women, as opposed to sex discrimination.[49] This draws attention to the vulnerabilities specific to women and not in comparison to men." Particular forms of discrimination are not stated, instead all forms are prohibited. The Convention specifies measures for the advancement and empowerment of women in private and public life, particularly in the areas of education, employment, health, marriage and the family.[50] The Convention acknowledges "the full and complete development of a country, the welfare of the world and the cause of peace require the maximum participation of women on equal terms with men in all fields."[51] The Treaty was a breakthrough for feminist discourse in a number of respects. The definition of discrimination against women was the first legally binding test articulated at the international level.[52]

One of the major breakthrough of the Convention is the declaration of women's rights as "human rights" Further it does not categorize them into first or second generation rights. Parties to CEDAW shall take all appropriate measures: "to modify the social and cultural patterns of conduct of men and women, with a view to achieving the elimination of prejudices and customary and all other practices which are based on the idea of the inferiority or the superiority of either of the sexes or on stereotyped roles for men and women" [53] and to "eliminate discrimination against women in rural areas in order to ensure, on a basis of equality of men and women, that they participate in and benefit from rural development". [54] The Convention was the first intenational instrument to identify the reasons for the subordinate role of women is society. The convention targeted tradition and culture as the factors shaping the roles and responsibilities in society. This is significant as such it was thought to be the subject matter of sociology and not law. The convention brought reason to the fore front of International law. The duty of law is not to merely proclaim and identify goals but also to identify the causes and rectify it. Then the law would be a significant step towards the elimination of gender based violence.[55]

Further convention sought to improve the position of women in family matters. It brought to the forefront the concept of right to health of women for the first time in human right agenda. Convention declares women's access to adequate health care facilities, including information, counselling and services in family planning" and "obtain all types of training and education, formal and non-formal, including that relating to functional literacy".[56]

Further convention empowers parties to take all appropriate measures to eliminate discrimination against women in all matters relating to marriage and family relations". In fact declaration reiterates the stand taken by earlier predecessors of Human Right Conventions. This includes: the "right freely to choose a spouse and to enter into marriage only with their free and full consent" and "to have access to the information, education and means to enable them to exercise these rights" and "the same rights for both spouses in respect of the ownership, acquisition, management, administration, enjoyment and disposition of property" The convention explicitly prohibits child marriage which is common practice in various traditional and religious societies.[57]

Another noteworthy aspect of the convention the convention extends the ambit of international human rights law to the 'private' arena. The significance of this is overwhelming. Women excessively endure human rights abuses committed outside the glare of public inspection. The Convention not only prohibits discriminatory practices by state officials, as is the general case with every other human rights treaty. However, Article 2(e) of the convention obliges States parties to "take al1 appropriate measures to eliminate discrimination in public and private spheres.[58] Article 2(e) does not make private persons internationally accountable for their wrongs. The responsibility is borne by the state.

CEDAW represents a big step forward in the promotion of women's rights. It contributes to the codification of human rights law in specifying the principle of equality enshrined in the Universal Declaration of Human Rights[59] and it is "the definitive international legal instrument requiring respect for, and observance of, the human rights of women; it is universal in reach, comprehensive in scope and legally binding in character." [60] The definition of discrimination goes beyond the usual idea of granting equal treatment and positively analyses the predicament of all-encompassing gender hierarchies and the inferior status of women in all spheres of life.

In spite of its comprehensiveness and universal nature the convention suffers from certain drawbacks which effect its functioning. Firstly in it's over enthusiasm to create a document that is agreeable to all parties resulted in various weakness and vagueness. It is to be noted that It is impossible to reach a consensus on a matter as sensitive and controversial as the rights of women. Further, Convention only refers to violence against women by implication. It fails to explicitly refer to violence as a human rights abuse or at least as a form of discrimination. The concept of state responsibility is conspicuously missing from the convention. Various fundamental flaws further dilute the effectiveness of the Women's Convention. The concept of reservation seriously cripples the convention. Reservations to the Women's Convention are numerous and pervasive. [61] It is unfortunate that most of the reservations directly affect the heart of the Treaty."[62] Generally speaking, CEDAW started as a weak human rights instrument that has developed increasing visibility and authority during its time of functioning from 1981.

Vienna Conference on Human Rights

If CEDAW brought a revolutionary progress in the recognition of women's rights, The Second World Conference on Human Rights changed the face of human rights forever. The world finally sat up and listened to the realization that the inferior status of women hampers the progress of society.[63] In Vienna, the message that "violence against women violates human rights" came through loud and clear.

"The full and equal participation of women in political, civil, economic, social and cultural life, at the national, regional and international levels, and eradication of all forms of discrimination on grounds of sex are priority objectives of the international community." [64] The above statement from the Vienna Declaration loudly proclaimed that women are part of the body of universal human rights.

It advanced the introduction of new human rights instruments, The Conference called for

(1) Universal ratification of the Women's Convention by the year 2000

(2) A complaints procedure for the Women's Convention;

(3) Withdrawal of extensive reservations to the Women's Convention;

(4) Appointment of a special rapporteur on violence against women

(5) Adoption of the Draft Declaration on the Elimination of Violence against Women (accomplished in 1994);

(6) Appointment of a High Commissioner of Human Rights

(8) Integration of women and mechanisms particular to women into the mainstream Human Rights agenda; and

(9) An end to gender based violence in al1 its forms and in ail areas of life. Vienna was simply a landmark for women.[65]

The focus all these years was the women's human rights in terms of political, social, economic and cultural rights. Significant achievements were achieved in advancing these rights with the focus on discrimination, violence and development. This approach was not sufficient to cater to the needs of a society were scientific and technological developments were taking place at a breathtaking speed. It is said Human Rights are always expanding and entering new horizon. Society slowly woke up to the possible adverse impact and probable human right violations.[66]

Science and Technology: New Threats to Women's Rights

The accelerated progress of science and technology is indisputable, as is its impact on economic, social, and cultural aspects. Already Unprecedented and invaluable advancements were achieved. The existence and uses of new technologies are changing how different women and men experience the world, the choices they make, and the work they do. New technologies impact women's lives all over the world. Advancements in science and technology have so far proved a mixed blessing with respect to the protection of human rights.

For instance, cheaper and more efficient means of communication which have evolved over the past 20 to 30 years have served to increase the flow of information across borders of all kinds: geographical, political, industrial, and interpersonal. Thus the right to freedom of expression and, in particular, the right to information is enhanced. However, it must be acknowledged that the same advances in technology that afford human beings greater access to information also permit governments, political parties, and other bureaucrats to gain even tighter control of that information. Furthermore, the relative ease with which information can now be communicated almost instantaneously to wide audiences heightens the dangers posed by the dissemination of faulty or distorted information, i.e. disinformation.[67]

New technologies specially impact women's lives all over the world. As future science and biotechnology, in the form of stem cell research, cloning, genetic testing and engineering and reproductive genetic technologies, besides offering several benefits in the form of preventive medicine and easy diagnosis poses serious human right threats to women. Women's bodies and women's eggs are the raw materials of these new human biotechnologies - what forms of violence are they, and will they perpetuate against women, and against future generations.[68] In fact these technologies are considered important tools for development, meaning they are increasingly presented as key components of solutions to long-standing problems like hunger, poverty, and environmental degradation. The technologies themselves have the promise of "fixing" these endemic problems or enhancing lives and livelihoods, but many of them pose threats to women's rights when utilized alongside powerful global forces.

The progress in science and technology is expected to have an impact on certain very basic rights Including right to life, and dignity, biology, medicine, gene technology, and nuclear technology, can determine or influence birth and death.

Problems posed by abortion, in vitro fertilization, embryo transplantation, euthanasia techniques, are examples. Further the developments in recording, surveillance devices, personality tests, and other communication techniques based on electronics, optics, and acoustics, as well as new reproduction techniques and biotechnological aids will considerably change the ways in which women's privacy could be protected.

Further along with challenges to human Rights significant questions arises in relation to access to these technologies and the right to enjoy the benefit of these technologies .Since Science and Technological progress is also reflective of societal conditions women are generally been kept out of the enjoyment of this right. Thus these developments are transforming the efforts for gender equality and presenting new challenges to women's rights.

Legal Response and Incorporation of Women's Concerns

The earlier Human Right declarations and treaties established by the international human rights instruments does not deal with science directly and targets the adverse effects of scientific and technological developments.

Despite the great amount of discussion on the impact of science and technology on human rights, the normative response resulting from it is relatively is meager. The international norms established to counter the effects of scientific and technological progress on human rights are often scattered among different kinds of other human rights problems such as torture and medical ethics, or find themselves as vague references in the declarations concerning welfare or development in general. The right to enjoy the benefits of scientific progress and its applications is included in the Universal Declaration of Human Rights [69]and the International Covenant on Economic, Social and Cultural Rights.[70] It is generally agreed that this right has not received adequate attention by the international human rights community. Some other indirect measures and provisions can be found in the provisions on human experimentation that form part of international humanitarian law.[71] These provisions lay emphasis on free and informed consent with regard to scientific practices. These provisions are contained in the 1949 Geneva Conventions.[72] The slow and indirect approach assumed by these instruments has prevented them from keeping pace with rapid developments in scientific understanding and technology.

The only international human rights instrument specifically related to scientific and technological progress is the Declaration on the Use of Scientific and Technological Progress in the Interest of Peace and for the Benefit of Mankind 1975, which expresses the wish that all states make use of scientific and technological progress for good purposes.[73] Specifically declaration enjoins the states to take the necessary measures, including legislative measures, to ensure that the utilization of scientific and technological achievements promotes the fullest realization of human rights and fundamental freedoms without any discrimination whatsoever on grounds of race, sex, language or religious beliefs. Further States should take effective measures, including legislative measures, to prevent and preclude the utilization of scientific and technological achievements to the detriment of human rights and fundamental freedoms and the dignity of the human person.[74]

It can be safely said, United Nations woke up to the potential threat of Science and Technology in 1968. The earliest text to focus on the adverse effects of new technological developments came out through the Teheran Declaration. [75] The declaration noted that scientific and technological projects "may ... endanger the rights and freedoms of individuals and will require continuing attention."[76] The more important is that the International Conference on Human Rights also passed a very specific resolution recognizing that scientific and technological developments "may entail certain dangers for the rights of the individual or for the group and for human dignity."[77] At the regional level In the first place, the signature of the Council of Europe's Convention for the Protection of Human Rights and Dignity of the Human Being with Regard to the Application of Biology and Medicine on April 4, 1997,[78] marked the emergence of specifically European response to the threat of science and technology inspired by the general principles of the European Convention on Human Rights.[79] It should be remembered that none of these instruments emphasis or stresses on the special threat the growing science and technology poses to women. Regarding India In contradistinction to what appears to characterize the western developed countries experience regarding scientific and genetic laws India has chosen not to recognize "Scientific exceptionality," To date we have refrained from crafting any distinctive legislative mechanism to deal with the use and misuse of scientific and technological information.

Internationally it can be concluded that the human rights aspects of scientific and technological developments have attracted little attention. The Universal Declaration on the *Human Genome* and *Human Rights* endorsed by the U.N. General Assembly on December 9, 1998, [80] is the first universal, instrument to establish an ethical and legal framework in the area of Scientific and specially Human Genome Project (HGP) research. The main idea that fuels the Declaration is that there is inherent dignity, and equal and inalienable rights bestowed in all members of the human family. The declaration prohibits genetic discrimination and emphasize on access to information. Through out the declaration, rights has been given a gender neutral definition and unfortunately women's concern does not find much attention. It provide no substantial provisions to enable women's to fight against the deprivation of social goods on genetic and medical grounds. The approach adopted by the Declaration is therefore too narrow to guard effectively against the potentially adverse impact that the HGP could have on the structure and composition of society especially on women.[81]

As a follow up to the declaration and to comprehensively relate bioethical issues and human rights, Declaration on Bioethics and Human Right was passed.[82] The Declaration addresses its provisions to states, and its scope comprises "ethical issues related to medicine, life sciences and associated technologies as applied to human beings." Its aims are, inter alia, to provide a framework of principles to guide states in the formulation of bioethics legislation and policies; to promote respect for human dignity and protect human rights; to foster pluralistic dialogue about bioethical issues; to promote equitable access to medical, scientific, and technological developments with particular attention to the needs of developing states; and to underline the importance of biodiversity. [83] The Declaration requires respect for the following principles: human dignity and human rights; maximization of benefit and minimization of harm to patients, research participants, and other affected individuals; autonomy and individual responsibility; informed consent to medical intervention and scientific research; special protection for persons without the capacity to consent; human vulnerability and personal integrity; privacy and confidentiality; equality, justice, and equity; non-discrimination and non-stigmatization; cultural diversity and pluralism; solidarity and cooperation; social responsibility and health; the sharing of benefits from scientific research; protection of future generations; and protection of the environment, the biosphere, and biodiversity. "in the interest of public safety, for the investigation, detection and prosecution of criminal offences, for the protection of public health or for the protection of the rights and freedoms of others." Again the language of the declaration is in gender neutral terminology. The only explicit provision on women relates to health. Art 14(2) guarantees access to quality health care and essential medicines, especially for the health of women and children, because health is essential to life itself and must be considered to be a social and human good;"

Conclusion

Rapid technological developments are in fact putting great strains on the law and its ability to adapt to new realities and challenges. One particularly pressing need of the time is to assess the role that international law and especially international human rights can play in developing a generally acceptable framework which will protect and promote women's rights in wake of the developments in new science and technology. [84]

The use of science and technological progress has a problematic history, and sadly, women have not fared well in that history. Science and Gender have sometimes proven to be an explosive and even fatal mixture. In Germany, for example, racial and ethnic minorities paid with their lives when developments in science were used in the service of a racial hygiene whose leaders gave enthusiastic and vocal support to Nazism. Groups such as Jews, Gypsies, and Slavs were targeted for extermination on the grounds that their genes posed a threat to the overall health and reproductive well-being of the German people. [85] In their tactics to exterminate these ethnic minorities' women were the worst sufferers because they are supposed to be the carriers of life and civilization.

As our capabilities for genetic screening, genetic engineering, Cloning, and other enhancement increase, we are likely to encounter more difficult ethical questions, including questions about the limits of autonomy, questions of eugenics, privacy and confidentiality laws. It is important not to become absorbed with exaggerated fears that the Science and technological development will foster a drive for the callous abuses and violation of women's human rights. Scientific research should continue because from the ethical point of view science and knowledge is independent of possible dexterous applications. Thus the need of the hour is to focus on the genuine social, ethical, and policy issues—some of them already evident—that various scientific inventions raises in relation to women's rights and to respond to them by creating codes of law and/or regulation for the use of these technologies by the media, insurers, employers, and the government itself.[86] Any policy response on this volatile and sensitive issue must remember that gender based violence and discrimination is an affront to human dignity. It is a threat to international peace and security, while its persistence will hamper human progress.[87]

References

1 Abdu'l -Bahd, 1992 quoted in A. Funder "De Minimis Non Curat Lex: The Clitoris, Culture and the Law" (1993) 3 Transnational Law & Contemporary Problems 4 17 at 42 1,(1993).

2 WHO A Global View of Violence Againstr Wornen in F. Hosken 'Wornen and Violence" 22-2 WIN News 5 1 at 51,(1996).

3 Janne Elisabeth Nijman, "The Concept Of International Legal Personality: An Inquiry Into The History And Theory Of International law" T.M.C. Asser Press, 2004.

4 Fali S. Nariman, "The Universality of Human Rights," 50 Rev. Int'l Commission Jurists 8, 11 (1993).

5 Magna Carta required King John of England to proclaim certain rights and that his will could be bound by the law. It explicitly protected certain rights of the King's subjects, whether free or fettered — and implicitly supported what became the writ of habeas corpus, allowing appeal against unlawful imprisonment.

6 In the United States, the Bill of Rights is the name by which the first ten amendments to the United States Constitution are known.

7 Declaration of the Rights of Man and the Citizen", Lectures on Modern European Intellectual history", The History Guide, available on <http://www.historyguide.org/intellect/lecture12a.html> Last visited on 3-03-2009).

8 Slavery Convention 1926 60 LNTS 253 In the traditional sense slavery persists throughout the world, but women are enslaved in many different circumstances that go unnoticed; women are not free.

9 The United Nations is an international organization founded in 1945 after the Second World War by 51 countries committed to maintaining international peace and security, developing friendly relations among nations and promoting social progress, better living standards and human rights.

10 Id, Art 1.

11 Id is a functional commission of the United Nations Economic and Social Council (ECOSOC), dedicated exclusively to gender equality and advancement of women. It is the principal global policy-making body. Every year, representatives of Member States gather at United Nations Headquarters in New York to evaluate progress on gender equality, identify challenges, set global standards and formulate concrete policies to promote gender equality and advancement of women worldwide.

12 Id available on< http://www.un.org/womenwatch/daw/csw/index.html>Last visited on 5-05-2009.

13 Marjorie Agosín, Women, Gender and Human Rights: A Global Perspective, Rutgers University Press, P141 (2001).

14 Universal Declaration of Human Rights, G.A. Res. 217A(III), U.N. GAOR, 3d Sess., at 71, U.N. Doc. A/810 (1948).

15 Tack Donelly ,The Relative Universality of Human Rights, 607 (1986).

16 The Concept of 'Generations' as opposed to categories' or 'catalogues is accredited to Stephen P. Marks. "Emerging Human Rights: A New Generation for the 80s, in R. Falk. International Law A Contemporas, Perspective, Westview Press, 504(1985).

17 Franziska Hosken, Women and International Human Rights - Toward a Definition of Women's Rights, 3 (1981).

18 Year Book Of The United Nations, Vol 50, Department of Public Information, New York (1996).

19 Id.

20 Supra Note 14 See Declaration of Human Rights.

21 Id (1) Men and women of full age, without any limitation due to race, nationality or religion, have the right to marry and to found a family. They are entitled to equal rights as to marriage, during marriage and at its dissolution. (2) Marriage shall be entered into only with the free and full consent of the parties.

22 Id Art 25.

23 Id, Preamble.

24 Id Art 21(3).

25 Convention on the Political Rights of Women, The Convention was adopted by the General Assembly in 1952 and entered into force on July 7, 1954.

26 Id Art 3.

27 This is the Recommendation on Consent to Marriage, Minimum Age

for Marriage and Registration of Marriages which is the General Assembly resolution 2018 (XX) of 1 November 1965.

28 (G.A. res. 2200A (XXI), 21 U.N.GAOR Supp (No. 16) at 49, U.N. Doc. A/6316 (1966), 993 .N.T.S. 3,entered into force Jan. 3, 1976.

29 International Covenant on Civil and Political Rights, G.A. res. 2200A (XXI), 21 U.N. GAOR Supp. (No. 16) at 52, U.N. Doc. A/6316 (1966).

30 Supra note 28 Art 3.

31 Id Art 7(a)(1).

32 Id Art 10(2).

33 Id Art 2 (2).

34 Supra note 29 Art 7(5).

35 Id Art 23(2).

36 Id Art 14.

37 Id Art 2.1.

38 Id Art 19.

39 Id. Article 2 of the ICCPR provides that "... {E}ach State Party to the present Covenant undertakes to take the necessary steps ... to adopt such legislative or other measures as may be necessary to give effect to the rights recognized in the present Covenant."

40 Id. Protocol to the ICCPR conventions Article I provides that A State Party to the Covenant that becomes a Party to the present Protocol recognizes the competence of the Committee to receive and consider communications from individuals subject to its jurisdiction who claim to be victims of a violation by that State Party of any of the rights set forth in the Covenant. No communication shall be received by the Committee if it concerns a State Party to the Covenant which is not a Party to the present Protocol.

41 Supra note 18 United Nations 1996.

42 UN Doc. E/ CN.6/ 575/ Rev. 1).

43 United Nations Development Fund for Women, New York,(1999).

44 Womens Rights are Human Rights , Fact Sheet Amnesty International USA.

45 Helen Jones, Watcing over the Rights of Women, Social policy and society, Vol. 5, No. 1, p. 127-136,(2006).

46 Year Book of United Nations, Department of Public Information(1975).

47 Starting in 1975, the International Women's Conference was started by the U.N. Since then, there have been four successful conferences that address the obstacles blocking the advancement of women.It

started with Mexico in 1975,followed by Copenhagen, Neirobi and Beijing.

48 UN GA Res 34/180, UN Doc A/34/46, 19 I.L.M. 33(1980).

49 Id Art 1 For the purposes of the present Convention, the term "discrimination against women" shall mean any distinction, exclusion or restriction made on the basis of sex which has the effect or purpose of impairing or nullifying the recognition, enjoyment or exercise by women, irrespective of their marital status, on a basis of equality of men and women, of human rights and fundamental freedoms in the political, economic, social, cultural, civil or any other field.

50 Id Art 10, 11 & 12.

51 Id preamble.

52 R. Cook, "State Accountability Under the Women's Convention" in R. Cook, ed., Human Rights of Women National and Iternational Perspectives, University of Pennsylvania Press, 228. (1994).

53 Id Article.

54 Id Art 14.

55 Preliminary report of the Special rapporteur on violence against women to the Commission on Human Rights UN Doc. E/CN.4/1995/422 2 November 1994 para i 10.

56 Supra note 47 Introduction.

57 Id Art 16.

58 Id Art 2(e).

59 Universal Declaration of Human Rights, G.A. Res. 217A (III), U.N. GAOR, 3d Sess., at 71, U.N. Doc. A/810, 1948.

60 Supra note 51 see Cook.

61 One-third of states parties have submitted reservations to the Women's Convention. K. Tomasevski Women and Humun Rights (Zed Books, 1993) at 117.

62 One of the most common reservations is invoking religious laws adhered to by the state concerned. Bangladesh, Libya, Tunisia and Egypt have utilized Islam as their reason for reserving provisions of the Treaty. The legal rulings under Islam are called the sharia. If any provision in the Women's Convention is contrary to the sharia, the sharia takes precedence. Many requirements of the sharia maintain women in a low status in society i.e. contradictory to the very raison d'erre of the Convention.

63 Vienna Conference on Human Rights A/CONF.157/24 (Part I) On 25 June 1993, representatives of 171 States adopted by consensus the

Vienna Declaration and Programme of Action of the World Conference on Human Rights.

64 Id Vienna Declaration and Programme of Action at part I Para 8.

65 Id.

66 Charlotte Bunch, International Networking for Women's Human Rights, Global Citizen Action, Ch 16.

67 United Nations. Human Rights: A Compilation of International Instruments. 1988. (ST/HR/1/ Rev 3.

68 Sujatha Jesudason,The future of Violence Against women :Human Rights and New Genetics available on <http://www.womensfunding network.org/resource/past-articles/the-future-of-violence-against-women-human-rights-the-new-genetics> Last visited on 3-05-2009).

69 Supra note 14 See UDHR Art 27 provides Everyone has the right freely to participate in the cultural life of the community, to enjoy the arts and to share in scientific advancement and its benefits. (2) Everyone has the right to the protection of the moral and material interests resulting from any scientific, literary or artistic production of which he is the author.

70 Supra note 28 Art 15.

71 Sev S. Fluss, The evolution of research ethics: the current international configuration, 32 J.L. Med. & Ethics 596, (2004).

72 The Geneva Conventions and their Additional Protocols are part of international humanitarian law – a whole system of legal safeguards that cover the way wars may be fought and the protection of individuals. available at <http://www.icrc.org/Web/Eng/siteeng0.nsf/htmlall/genevaconventions>visited on 14-01-2008).

73 Declaration on the Use of Scientific and Technological Progress in the Interests of Peace and for the Benefit of Mankind, A/RES/30/3384 Declaration states All States shall take measures to extend the benefits of science and technology to all strata of the population and to protect them, both socially and materially, from possible harmful effects of the misuse of scientific and technological developments, including their misuse to infringe upon the rights of the individual or of the group, particularly with regard to respect for privacy and the protection of the human personality and its physical and intellectual integrity.

74 Id.

75 Final Act of the International Conference on Human Rights, Teheran, 22 April to 13 May 1968, U.N. Doc. A/CONF.32/41.

76 Id. Res. 11 at 12.

77 Id.

78 European Convention on Human Rights and Biomedicine, Apr. 4, 1997, CETS No. 164, available at http:// conventions.coe.int/treaty/en/treaties/html/164.htm (last visited 3-07-2009) [hereinafter EU Convention]. Thirty-two countries are signatories to the convention.

79 The European Convention on Human Rights and Biomedicine has been ratified, as of January 1, 1999, by Greece, San Marino, Slovakia, and Slovenia. This convention will only enter into force, however, "on the first day of the month following the expiration of a period of three months after the date on which five States, including at least four member States of the Council of Europe, have expressed their consent to be bound by the Convention . . . ." European Convention on Human Rights and Biomedicine.

80 G.A. Res. 152, U.N. GAOR, 53d Sess., U.N. Doc. A/53/625/Add.2 (1998) (hereinafter U.N. General Assembly Resolution on the Human Genome Declaration) (adopting Universal Declaration on the Human Genome and Human Rights, available online at <http:// www.unesco.org/ibc/uk/genome/projet/index.html> (visited 20-04-2009.

81 Id.

82 U.N. Educ., Sci., & Cultural Org. [UNESCO], Universal Declaration on Bioethics and Human Rights, General Conference of UNESCO, 33rd sess. avvailable at http://portal.unesco.org/shs/en/file_download.php/46133e1f4691e4c6e57566763d474a4dBioethic_EN.pdf .(last visited on 4-04-2009).

83 Anna Gercas, The Universal Declaration on Bioethics and Human Rights: Promoting International Discussion on the Morality of Non-Therapeutic Research on Children, 27 Mich. J. Int'l l. 629,(2005).

84 Francesco Francioni, Genetic Resources, Biotechnology and Human Rights: The International Legal Framework, European University Institute Law Working Paper No. 2006/17.

85 Arthur L. Caplan, Race, Ethnicity, Class, and Genetics—a Grim and Dismal History available at R. Proctor, Racial Hygiene: Medicine under the Nazis, Cambridge, Mass.: Harvard University Press, (1988).

86 Id.

87 c. Bunch "'Violence Against Women and Girls: the Intolerable Status Quo" in UNICEF. The Progress of Nations 1997 quoted F. Hosken 'Women and Violence" 23-4, (1997).

2

Human Genome Project and Genetic Testing: Safeguarding Gender Genetic Privacy

Introduction

"The struggle for human rights is like an overflowing river that floods down across the valley making the fields ever more fertile" With this simile, an Italian academic illustrates the expanding force of the human rights movement, which tends to cover all new areas in which the dignity and freedom of the human person is in need of protection. Probably the most recent field that needs to be "fertilized" by the principles of human rights is medicine, especially genetics. The progress in Genetics marked a turning point with the culmination of Human genome Project. (Hereinafter HGP)Rapid advances in this area present new and complex ethical and policy issues for individuals and society, and a legal response is needed to avoid misuse of the new technologies.[1] This chapter describes the potential impact of the "new genetics" on women. This chapter specially deals with the issue of gender privacy in genetic testing.

DNA: Basic Science

Since the beginning of the history human beings have wondered how traits are inherited from one generation to the next. It took them centuries of knowledge seeking to realise the role of genes in transmitting the traits. Genes carry the information to create all of the proteins required by every organism.[2] These proteins determine, among other things, how the organism looks, how the body fights infection and how it behaves. Essentially, genetic information provides the framework for an individual's traits.[3]

Genes have played a role in the composition of life since the dawn of time; however, it was not until recently that man has discovered them. The history of modern genetics began in 1863 when Gregor Mendel, in his study of peas, discovered that traits are transmitted from parents to progeny by independent units called genes.[4] Close to one century later, Oswald Avery, Colin MacLeod, and Maclyn McCarty published a paper describing the transforming principle of genetic material as DNA, beginning the era of molecular genetics.[5] One of the largest discoveries in the field of genetics, the discovery of the double helical structure of DNA occurred in 1953 and is attributed to Watson and Crick.[6] DNA constitutes the molecules inside cells that carry genetic information and pass it from one generation to the next.[7] DNA is made up of 4 bases (adenine, guanine, cytosine, and thymine) which are each bonded to a sugar (deoxyribose) and a phosphate to make nucleotides. These are repeated in various sequences along the molecule. Complementary bases pair to form a double helix structure. The sequence of nucleotides makes a gene which is used to make proteins.[8] A genome is an organism's complete set of DNA, including all of its genes. Each genome contains all of the information needed to build and maintain that organism. In humans, a copy of the entire genome—more than 3 billion DNA base pairs—is contained in all cells that have a nucleus.[9] In the past half century, the field of molecular genetics has progressed at an unbelievably rapid rate. [10] The climax of the genetic revolution occurred when the entire human genome was sequenced and published in 2003.[11]

Human Genome Project

At the forefront of the biology movement is the Human Genome Project, a 13-year project coordinated by the U.S. Department of Energy and the National Institutes of Health federally funded mission to determine the sequence of human DNA.[12]

Project goals were to

- *identify* all the approximately 20,000-25,000 genes in human DNA,
- *determine* the sequences of the 3 billion chemical base pairs that make up human DNA,
- *store* this information in databases,
- *improve* tools for data analysis,
- *transfer* related technologies to the private sector, and
- *Address* the ethical, legal, and social issues (ELSI) that may arise from the project.[13]

The fascinating story of HGP began in the mid 1980s after Fred Sanger had successfully demonstrated in 1977, that double stranded DNA could be sequenced using the dideoxy sequencing technique.[14] During the mid 80s there was considerable excitement both in scientific as well as public circles about the possibility of sequencing the whole genome of humans. The practicality of such an undertaking was discussed at two meetings, one at Santa Cruz, USA in 1985 [15] and another year later at Santa by Renato Dulbecco. Realizing the potential of such an effort, two Government agencies of the United States – Department of Energy (DOE) and the National Institute of Health (NIH) in 1988, drafted the first proposal to 'coordinate research and technical activities related to the human genome'.[16] HGP thus kicked off in 1990. The first period was between 1990 to 1995 and second between 1998-2003

The progress report of that period and final projections was announced five years later in 1998.[17] The project evolved over the 90s decade and in its final stages had over 16 international centers involved globally in the task of sequencing all the human chromosomes.[18] The major landmarks during this process were on December 2, 1999, more than 100 scientists working together in laboratories in the United Kingdom, Japan, the United States, Canada, and Sweden announced the first completely sequenced human chromosome 22, the smallest of the autosomes. To assure the accuracy of the sequenced data, each segment was sequenced at least ten times.[19] Next landmark was the publication of the human genomic map. On Monday, June 26 2000 The International Human Genome Sequencing Consortium published the first draft of the human genome in the journal *Nature* in February 2001.[20] The Draft of HGP has revealed that there are probably somewhere between 30,000 and 40,000 human genes. The high-quality reference sequence was completed in April 2003, marking the end of the Human Genome Project two years ahead of the original schedule.

In April 2003, researchers announced that the Human Genome Project had completed a high-quality sequence of essentially the entire human genome. This sequence closed the gaps from a working draft of the genome, which was published in 2001. It also identified the locations of many human genes and provided information about their structure and organization. The Project made the sequence of the human genome and tools to analyze the data freely available via the Internet. [21] Though the HGP is finished, analyses of the data will continue for many years. Rapid progress in genome science and a glimpse into its potential applications have spurred observers to predict that biology will be the foremost science of the 21st Century. The completion of the Human Genome

Project opens up a wealth of knowledge with the possibility of understanding the simple, yet essential, components of our being; DNA and the genes encoded within. The scientific and medical communities are presently working to decipher this monumental discovery and integrate the information into their pre-existing data. Once the function of each gene and protein in the human genome has been determined, scientists, researchers and doctors will possess the capability to make advances in bioinformatics, analyze and produce effective drugs more efficiently and economically, create novel cures for genetic diseases, and, or, possibly remove genetic defect.[22] Technology and resources generated by the Human Genome Project and other genomic research already are having major impacts on research across the life sciences.[23]

Various ethical and legal issues also comes to forefront in any discussion on HGP including

- Privacy and fairness in the use of genetic information, including the potential for genetic discrimination in employment and insurance.
- The integration of new genetic technologies, such as genetic testing, into the practice of clinical medicine.
- Ethical issues surrounding the design and conduct of genetic research with people, including the process of informed consent.
- The education of healthcare professionals, policy makers, students, and the public about genetics and the complex issues that result from genomic research.[24]

An international study in 19 nations has shown that human genetics and their patients frequently face a set of ethical problems including fairness of access to genetic services, abortion choices, confidentiality problems, and disclosure dilemmas in counseling; screening policies etc. [25] These issues can ultimately be grouped into issues pertaining to genetic testing, and screening.[26] Developments in HGP will have far reaching effects on society, but at the same time it has to be observed and remembered that all effects of HGP is not equally divided between man and women. Women due to the central role they play in reproduction, family health are particularly affected differently. The plight and agony of women get aggravated by the low social and economic position they enjoy.

Genetic Testing

There is no universally accepted definition of what constitutes a genetic test.[27] Gene tests, are generally utilized to check for genetic disorders. In genetic testing an analysis of DNA, chromosomes, or gene products to provide specific information about variations in the number or form of genes or chromosomes in an individual or his or her progeny is undertaken. The newest and most sophisticated genetic tests involve direct examination of the DNA molecule.[28] Genetic tests use a variety of laboratory techniques to determine if a person has a genetic condition or disease or is likely to get the disease. The genetic change can be relatively large: a missing or added piece of a chromosome, a change in position of a part or the entire chromosome - that is visible under a microscope. Such a study of chromosomes is called as Cytogenetics[29] If the genetic change is extremely small, as little as one extra, missing, or altered chemical base at the level of single gene it is called a molecular defect. The testing of such disorders is called Molecular genetics or DNA testing.[30] These genetic testing fall under various categories.

Types of Genetic Testing

Diagnostic Testing

Diagnostic testing is used to identify or rule out a specific genetic or chromosomal condition. Using various technologies the genetic information of an individual is probed for defects or variants in one or more genes to confirm or exclude a specific disease diagnosis. In many cases, genetic testing is used to confirm a diagnosis when a particular condition is suspected based on physical signs and symptoms. Diagnostic testing can be performed before birth or at any time during a person's life, but is not available for all genes or all genetic conditions. The results of a diagnostic test can influence a person's choices about health care and the management of the disorder.[31]

Carrier Testing

Carrier testing is used to identify people who carry one copy of a gene mutation that, when present in two copies, causes a genetic disorder. These tests are usually done for diseases with a strictly genetic basis, either before or after birth. This type of testing is offered to individuals who have a family history of a genetic disorder and to people in certain ethnic groups with an increased risk of specific genetic conditions. If both parents are tested, the test can provide information about a couple's risk of having a child with a genetic condition.[32]

Predictive Testing

Predictive DNA testing offers the possibility of detecting many gene mutations associated with disorders that appear after birth, often later in life that have a genetic basis, such as cancer. This test can be helpful to people who have a family member with a genetic disorder, but who have no features of the disorder at the time of testing. However, a genetic alteration might only indicate susceptibility to or a high risk of developing a disease, but not the certainty of having or developing it.[33]

Presymptomatic Tests

The presence of defects in certain specific genes or gene products creates an almost 100% risk of developing a particular disease later in life. Presymptomatic testing can determine whether a person will develop a genetic disorder. Huntington's chorea, Hereditary Polyposis Coli carcinoma ,some rare forms of Alzheimer's disease, and some forms of familial hereditary thyroid carcinoma are the diseases most frequently tested for in genetic centre's under this category.[34] The tests in this category cover a broad range of diseases and acquired conditions and can lead to the prediction of the future health status of an individual. However, the dividing line between strictly inherited and acquired conditions is not always clearly defined.

Various genetic tests are developed and followed. For instance Since the 1960s pregnant women have been routinely tested for their rhesus blood group, [35]so that damage to babies of rhesus negative women before and after birth can be prevented. Damage is prevented by ensuring that rhesus negative women are given an antibody within a few hours of delivery, miscarriage or abortion. Since 1973 it has been policy to screen all newborn babies in the UK for phenylketonuria (PKU).[36] Severe mental retardation is characteristic of this disease, but can be prevented if dietary treatment is started in the first weeks of life.

Ethical and Legal Issues

Genetic testing has several advantages to its credit. It has drastically improved lives. Some tests are used to clarify physician toward appropriate treatments, while others allow families to avoid having devastating diseases or identify people at high risk conditions that may be prevented by proper monitoring and other treatment methodologies like genetic engineering. With all these promises it hold for the humanity genetic testing at the same time raises several ethical questions specially in relation to women.

The availability of genetic testing in society brings along with it issues of fairness and accessibility of these services.[37] Equality of opportunity and access is a fundamental social value which is especially damaged where a society is divided.[38] The genomics era may aggravate the "gender divide" various questions arises in relation to access of genetic services which consists of, who should be able to make use of genetic tests and interventions if they are developed? And who should bear the cost of the tests and interventions? But the anxiety, however is that if such tests and interventions were available for private purchase, The access to these tests will be limited to only more affluent members of society leading to even greater inequalities and increase social and economic polarization. The genetic testing existing today can not be accessible to common people and especially to females due to their social and economic dependence. From an egalitarian perspective, if these resources are not available to general public, then the tests and interventions should not be introduced at all. However, libertarians argue that there is no moral basis for this they believe that if a trait like athleticism is desirable and there is an intervention that will increase the likelihood of it occurring, the correct response is to ensure that it is available as widely as possible. While this may entail that, for at least a limited period of time, there will be some who do not have access; the overall goal should be to raise everyone to the highest level. It is difficult at this time to adjudicate in the abstract between these two view points. It is only once some effective intervention is under consideration that the costs and benefits of full public availability versus limited private availability for a privileged few can be assessed seriously.[39]

Further genetic testing also raises issues including potential psychological harm to the person being tested; ramifications for other family members; possible breaches of privacy; the risk of discrimination besides major concerns regarding the question of informed consent and confidentiality.

Informed Consent and Confidentiality

The seeking of consent is a process to ensure that a person understands the nature and purpose of giving a sample or undergoing an intervention. Generally, in medico-legal terms, 'valid consent' is ensured if anything that represents a significant risk that would affect the judgement of a reasonable person has been explained.[40] The requirement of consent flows from the concept of individual autonomy. The term autonomy is derived from the Greek words autos ("self") and nomos ("law" or "rule"). While there is no unifying definition of the principle of autonomy from the philosophical or ethical perspective, To make one's own choices—that is, for those choices to be autonomous—one must be unrestrained by unwarranted interference by others and should be in apposition to make one's own choices.[41] Although autonomy is concerned with choice and the exercise of that choice in relation to life decisions, realistically it must be accepted that no person can control, at all times, all aspects of his or her life.[42] This is specially true in the case of females who is subordinated socially and economically. In various societies even freedom of thoughts are denied to them. In such scenario it will be worthwhile to ponder how the requirement of informed consent and its application relating to women.

Responsible health authorities and legal systems make informed consent central. Legally, informed consent, has 'three discrete and equally important aspects: first, consent is only valid if the person giving it is competent to do so; second, the person giving consent must be properly informed; and third, the consent must be given voluntarily'. This is not simply a matter of signing a form, but an individual must be aware of the complexity of the decision.[43]

Women all over the world satisfy the first criteria of competency. Regarding the second criteria of consent be informed, it comes with education and awareness. If we analyze the general social conditions of women they suffer from lack of education and awareness. For instance Question arises with prenatal screening, is the mother really in a position to give informed consent to a fairly technical procedure that provides an indication of 'risk.'? Given their greater role in the childrearing process, women are often the ones who are expected to make the decisions about genetic testing specially in case of antenatal screening. Given that often this involves the careful evaluation of 'risk', this is not easy. As Murray and Botkin observe: "In screening programmes especially, though potentially also in presymptomatic screening, women typically bear a disproportionate burden. They often are tested first, with men tested later if at all; when decisions are made whether to continue a pregnancy, women must bear the direct consequences, whatever choice is made."[44] These arguments points that it will require extra effort and concern on the part of health care practioners while dealing the cases of women.

In the case of voluntary consent situation is controversial. In fact there is various evidence that social pressure can undermine the principle of informed and voluntary consent. Further Callahan writes "When prenatal diagnosis was being introduced in the late 1960s, every assurance was given that no woman would be forced to have such a diagnosis, much less be forced into an abortion if the diagnosis turned up a terrible genetic defect. The great anxiety focused on government coercion of those who would be judged unfit mothers. The worry about direct coercion was misplaced, but that did not mean influence was absent. Social pressure and developing mores on prenatal diagnosis soon turned into a routine 'medically indicated' procedure, as common and standard for women over the age of 35 as taking blood pressure. It takes a tough and determined woman these days to exercise the free choice' of not choosing prenatal diagnosis, and a still tougher and more determined woman not to have an abortion if a serious defect is discovered in her fetus after that diagnosis. Here, as elsewhere, social condition played a major part in any decisions.[45]

The nature of genetically linked illness ensures that among the most troubling concerns of a person considering genetic testing are likely to be: "What will this information reveal about me and my family"? And "What information should I disclose to my family? Although having a genetic trait for cancer is not contagious, learning that one has such a trait raises painful questions about disclosure to one's siblings, partner, children, and parents. Moreover, because genetic flaws are transmissible, a woman who wishes to bear children, but has not yet done so, faces complex dilemmas concerning the risk of transmission to her future children. If she already has children, she must confront difficult questions regarding disclosure to them, because they also may carry her genetic predisposition to the illness. The issue of confidentiality emerges as one of the critical aspect of genetic testing.

The doctrine of physician—patient confidentiality can be traced as far back as the fourth century B.C. to the Hippocratic Oath, which is still recited by medical students when they enter the medical profession.[46] The underlying reason for the physician's duty to maintain patient confidentiality is that it is necessary to ensure that patients freely divulge personal information, however sensitive, that is necessary for their treatment.[47] This deeply rooted doctrine is also codified in the Code of Medical Ethics of the American Medical Association (AMA), which provides in pertinent part that "[a] physician shall respect the rights of patients, colleagues, and other health professionals, and shall safeguard patient confidences and privacy within the constraints of the law." [48]

Regarding normal medical information the requirement of confidentiality does not lead to much of a problem except where non disclosure of information harms some ones interest. But question of confidentiality in the case of genetic information brings additional challenges. Genetic information differs from other forms of medical information because it pertains to a range of people and not solely to one individual. In this respect, it gives rise to special problems concerning how the information should be gathered, stored, accessed, and used. While one might choose to locate control of a genetic sample with the person from whom it has been taken, [49]one cannot ignore the fact that genetic information derived from the sample also reveals information about the relatives of the sample source Unlike most medical information, genetic information is inherently more than a matter for the individual – it is of relevance to families. In order to give accurate clinical information to an individual at risk for a genetic disorder, it is sometimes necessary to use medical data obtained from one or more members of that individual's family. Because of this, exchange of family information is inherent in medical genetics.[50]

Confidentiality is a central tenet of medicine, but in clinical genetics the family connection raises important questions of principle and practice. Is the duty of confidentiality owed to the individual who seeks medical information, or is it owed to the larger family? Should professionals feel duty-bound to inform other family members, even if they are unaware of any problem? In its report on genetic screening, the Nuffield Council on Bioethics argued that it may be appropriate to define the family as a 'unit' in relation to the use of genetic information. However, it also recognised that disclosure of genetic data within the family 'raises some of the most serious issues'.[51]

The disclosure that one is afflicted with, a carrier for, or genetically predisposed to contract a genetically determined disease can cause "devastating" emotional and psychological harm to an individual. [52] The testing can also cause "family strife," with some members "protesting the test itself so as not to open an investigation into the family's genetic reality." Finally, the revelation of genetic test results to family members may cause a special type of harm, one that some commentators have labeled the "family secrets" problem.[53] These problems can be aggravated in the case of females.

These fears are substantiated in the famous case of BRCA1 which revealed the dilemma faced by females in the case of genetic testing. BRCA1 is the gene responsible for between 5% and 10% of female breast cancers. It was discovered in 1994 and is known to be 10 times longer than most human genes.[54] This fact means that the likelihood of mutations is increased and this, in turn, has implications for the efficacy of test kits designed to identify the gene, for they cannot detect all mutations. There is a high risk of secondary cancers associated with this disease, but early detection and radical intervention in the form of mastectomy can reduce this risk. Preventative measures, also in the form of mastectomies, can reduce the instances of disease.[55]

Nicola is aware of a history of breast cancer in her family. Her mother, her great-grandmother, and one of her aunts died from the disease. Nicola has a sister, Nadia, and three female cousins, Norma, Romana, and Elvira. She does not know the extent to which these relatives are aware of the pattern of disease in the family. Nicola discovered a lump in her breast which has been diagnosed as malignant. She is concerned that the BRCA1 gene runs in her family and that her sister and cousins are at risk. Nicola's physician has advised a mastectomy and has strongly urged her to contact her relatives to arrange testing. Should she approach her sister and cousins with the news of her own disease and urge them to seek medical advice? She is aware, for example, that Nadia is phobic about operations and that Elvira is prone to bouts of depression.

The dilemma faced by women in genetic testing is clearly brought about in the case. Various points can be advanced in this case. In an extreme one can assume that the woman who has been diagnosed with breast cancer in our scenario is owed a duty of confidence by her health care professional. This entitles her to decide whether and how the information, which is the object of the duty, should be disclosed to others. On the other spectrum in the case of her relatives, it would be possible for the health care professional to justify disclosing the information to them even without the patient's consent, because the duty of confidentiality is not absolute, and certain exceptions are admitted, including actions to prevent harm to third parties.[56] In the case cited above, disclosure to female relatives may bring various positive benefits. The information may help them to undertake preventive measures.

Question arises whether same principle should be followed in all case of genetic testing involving women? The prevailing social and economic conditions of women suggest other wise.

If we take an analogy from HIV status in women and its disclosure, situation can be clear. Studies have proved that HIV testing can carry risks for women, including violence and stigma. Rates of non-disclosure are especially high among women seeking antenatal care. According to the Pan American Health Organization, not only are pregnant women more vulnerable and economically dependent, but pregnancy is a period of particularly high-risk for violence. Fearful of these risks, women tested may not disclose their HIV status to their partners. According to one study, an average of 71 percent of women in the developed world and only 52 percent of women in the developing world share their HIV status with their partners.[57]

Further in studies in sub-Saharan Africa and Southeast Asia, between 3.5 to 14.6 percent of women reported a violent reaction, blame, stigmatization abandonment, and loss of economic support. from their partner following disclosure of their HIV status. More or less same situation followed in a study in India, 12 out of 52 women who disclosed their results to their partner were beaten or abused by their in-laws, and 18 of 52 were no long allowed to do housework.[58]

Genetic information is not only an indicator of an individual's current state of health; it is also an indicator of that individual's likely future health. For medical conditions controlled by a single gene (such as Huntington's disease), the indication can be precise. For medical conditions that involve a more complex combination of genes or environmental factors (such as heart disease), the indication might involve only an increased probability that a future medical problem may arise.

Controlling genetic defects that would, otherwise, be passed on to future generations would appear to be a desirable goal. However, depending upon how broadly or narrowly the notion of a "defect" is construed, discrimination predicated upon genetic information may arise in more or less benign form. Indeed, if technology advances far enough to permit the medical alteration of an individual's genes, society may seek to weed out, whether by government regulation or by popular prejudice, the most egregious so-called genetic defects under the guise of benefitting future generations. In some circumstances, the individuals affected may find that the use of their personal genetic information by third parties is therapeutic or economically beneficial. In other circumstances, however, individuals inevitably will object to the use of their personal genetic information by third parties. The best defense against such use would be to establish a legal right to privacy over one's own genetic profile. As yet, however, there is no consensus regarding how much or how little privacy should be preserved.

Courts generally recognize a privilege to disclose medical information when such disclosure is necessary to protect the general public[59] or certain present or future family members of the patient. This duty to warn of communicable diseases and other known injuries was dramatically expanded in 1976 when the California Supreme Court handed down its landmark *Tarasoff* v. *Regents of the University of California* decision in which it imposed an affirmative duty on a psychotherapist to breach patient confidentiality in order to warn others of potential harm.[60] In its 1980 *Thompson* v. *County of Alameda*[61] decision, the California Supreme Court limited the category of potential victims to whom a therapist owes a Tarasoff duty to warn to those who are "readily identifiable."[62] The Tarasoff court found that a duty to warn probably exists if the physician has a special relationship with the person who may cause the harm of the potential victim, the potential victim or person at risk is identifiable, and the harm to the victim is foreseeable and serious.[63]

In *Schroeder* v. *Perkel*,[64] the first reported case involving genetic disclosure issues, the parents of two children born with cystic fibrosis brought a wrongful life action against the doctors who treated their first child, alleging that their negligent failure to diagnose the child's cystic fibrosis, a hereditary disease, deprived them of the ability to make an informed choice about having a second child.[65] The pediatricians contended that they owed no duty to the plaintiffs because the child, not her parents, was their patient. In rejecting this argument, the New Jersey Supreme Court noted that the scope of the physicians' duty in negligence was "coextensive with the reasonable foreseeability" of their negligence and that the likelihood of injury to family members of the patient had to be examined in light of the legal relationships among family members.[66]

The American Society of Human Genetics (ASHG), a professional organization for human geneticists in the Americas whose members include researchers, academicians, clinicians, laboratory professionals, genetic counselors, nurses, and others with special interest in human genetics,[67] has identified the following four ethical positions regarding a health care professional's duty or privilege to warn at-risk relatives about genetic information:

- The position that genetic information deserves absolute confidentiality,
- The position that the professional may (but is not required to) warn at-risk relatives if certain conditions are satisfied,
- The position that the patient should be warned—before genetic testing—about circumstances that would result in disclosure of genetic information to at-risk relatives, and
- The position that the health care professional has an ethical duty to warn at-risk relatives.[68] The professional

associations that have addressed this issue have taken various positions along the continuum of options outlined by the ASHG.[69] The National Society of Genetic Counselors' (NSGC) position statement on genetic information provides that the individual should have absolute control over who has access to his or her genetic information. [70]This position is consistent not only with the underlying philosophy of genetic counseling that patients should be permitted to independently determine the uses to which their genetic information is put.

International Legal Framework

Modern Human Right regime began with the establishment of United Nations. Over the Years U.N played a significant role in the development and codification of Human Right. The initial effort of elaborating the basic rights came through the adoption of Universal Declaration of Human Rights in 1948.[71] The Universal Declaration in clear terms laid down various fundamental rights which will ensure the dignity of Individual. The declaration was followed by The International Covenants on Civil and Political rights [72]and International Covenants on Economic, Social and Cultural Rights respectively.[73]

It should be noted that at the beginning the human right threat posed by the development in science and technology did not get much attention from the United Nations That was quite understandable given the fact that there were serious and other grave human right violations in the form of discrimination, slavery, torture etc to be taken care of . Still certain sections of international bill of Rights can be interpreted as catering to the threat posed by technological development sin society.

Article 27(1) of UDHR declares that: "Everyone has the right freely to participate in the cultural life of the community, to enjoy the arts and to share in scientific advancement and its benefit."[74] Besides this several other clauses could be interpreted to protect individuals from some of the HGP's potentially adverse social consequences. For example, Article 7 affirms the equality of all individuals before the law and provides equal protection against all forms of discrimination.[75] Article 25 implicitly recognizes a right to health, stating that "Everyone has the right to a standard of living adequate for the health and well-being of himself and his family."[76] A progressive reading of Article 25 would mean that individuals and women be given full access to the medical benefits generated by the HGP thus banning the use of genetic information in relation to insurance.

Art 15 of ICESCR states that everyone is "to enjoy the benefits of scientific progress and its applications" and that countries undertake to "respect the freedom indispensable for scientific research." [77] Article 12 might be read to ensure that women have access to genetic data and technologies. Significantly, Article 12(2) (d) seeks to ensure that health care will be available to all people: It imposes duty on the states which reads that States must ensure "the creation of conditions which would assure to all medical service and medical attention in the event of sickness."[78] Article 7 emphasizes that "No-one shall be subjected without their free consent to medical or scientific experimentation."[79] This clause forms the bedrock principle of informed consent under medical law and protects the human beings from undue interference and experimentation on them.[80] Though some provisions can be interpreted to have a correlation with the threat posed to human right by science and technology the declarations are conspicuous by its absence to explicitly declare any right. relating to women.

It can be safely said, United Nations woke up to the potential threat of Science and Technology in 1968.with the Teheran Declaration.[81] At present, two international legal instruments in the field of biomedicine are particularly noteworthy The UNESCO Universal Declaration on the Human

Genome and Human Rights [82] and at the European level, the Convention on Human Rights and Biomedicine, both of which were adopted in 1997.[83] These two instruments are just the first steps towards the elaboration of an international biomedical law:

The Declaration on Human Genome was drafted by the legal commission of UNESCO's International Bioethics Committee (hereinafter IBC), an independent body within UNESCO, a panel of forty independent experts charged with promoting the development of international instruments on the human genome, and finalized by a committee of intergovernmental experts. It is the first universal, rather than regional, instrument to establish an ethical framework for activities in this area, whether for research itself or for the application of findings. It is thus a vital part of the intense standard-setting activity that characterizes bioethics today. At the national level, a growing number of countries have enacted legislation on bioethical issues relating to genetic testing over the past twenty years, especially in Europe. For instance, legislation on new reproductive technologies and on embryo research was enacted in 1988 in Spain[84] and in 1990 in Germany[85] and in the United Kingdom.[86] Legally, the Access to Medical Reports Act 1988 states that disclosure of test results should be entirely at the discretion of the individual.[87]

The Human Genome Declaration does not seek to govern specific practices; rather, it spells out universally-accepted ethical principles. These principles are to guide researchers and medical practitioners as well as public and private decision-makers involved in fields relating to human genetics. The Human Genome Declaration is intended mainly for States that wish to draft bioethics legislation, as well as for members of the judiciary operating in a legal vacuum or interpreting their national legislation.

The declaration underlies the principles of human dignity. Article 10 says "No research or research applications concerning the human genome, in particular in the fields of biology, genetics and medicine, should prevail over respect for the human rights, fundamental freedoms and human dignity of individuals or, where applicable, of groups of people. "Further equality of access to genetic services are envisaged Article 12 (a) points to that "Benefits from advances in biology, genetics and medicine, concerning the human genome, shall be made available to all, with due regard for the dignity and human rights of each individual. clause (b)also lays down Freedom of research, which is necessary for the progress of knowledge, is part of freedom of thought. The applications of research, including applications in biology, genetics and medicine, concerning the human genome, shall seek to offer relief from suffering and improve the health of individuals and humankind as a whole"[88]

The relevant articles to the further discussion are Article 17 which encourages States to develop research designed to include the "prevention" of genetic disease. This can be interpreted as promoting and encouraging Genetic testing. Article 5 (a) covers the rights of those who undergo "research, treatment or diagnosis" on their own genome. It reads "Research, treatment or diagnosis affecting an individual's genome shall be undertaken only after rigorous and prior assessment of the potential risks and benefits pertaining thereto and in accordance with any other requirement of national law."[89]

Article 5(b) provides guidelines for research on the genome of a person unable to give consent. When this research is carried out not for the sake of any direct health benefit for the person, but in the interests of a third party, it is envisaged that such research will be carried out only "by way of exception, with utmost restraint. In all cases, the prior, free and informed consent of the person concerned shall be obtained. If the latter is not in a position to consent, consent or authorization shall be obtained in the manner prescribed by law, guided by the person's best interest. Article 5(c) affirms respect for the right of each person to decide whether or not to be informed of the results of a genetic examination.[90] Yet the right of the individual concerned cannot be absolute in this regard: there is a need to consider cases where this information has consequences for the health of other persons (e.g. family members). Regarding the requirement and concept of confidentiality Article 9 lays down "In order to protect human rights and fundamental freedoms, limitations to the principles of consent and confidentiality may only be prescribed by law, for compelling reasons within the bounds of public international law and the international law of human rights.[91]

More or less similar guidelines and principles can be found in The European Convention Special measures are envisaged to respect informed consent and confidentiality. Article 5 lays down "An intervention in the health field may only be carried out after the person concerned has given free and informed consent to it. This person shall beforehand be given appropriate information as to the purpose and nature of the intervention as well as on its consequences and risks. And the person concerned may freely withdraw consent at any time. in response to confidentiality requirement. [92] Convention further lays down that Tests which are predictive of genetic diseases or which serve either to identify the subject as a carrier of a gene responsible for a disease or to detect a genetic predisposition or susceptibility to a disease may be performed only for health purposes or for scientific research linked to health purposes, and subject to appropriate genetic counselling. Article 10 lays down "everyone has the right to respect for private life in relation to information about his or her health. Further Everyone is entitled to know any information collected about his or her health. However, the wishes of individuals not to be so informed shall be observed. In exceptional cases, restrictions may be placed by law on the exercise of the rights contained in paragraph 2 in the interests of the patient.[93]

The Declaration was a response to the dramatic and alarming rate of scientific advances, particularly genetic ones. Its conception was marked by several themes: fear that science would irreversibly damage a fundamental aspect of humanity; hope that a just society is within human capabilities; and concern that we are far from that society and sliding in the wrong direction. Despite the negative triggers, it was a response by a body (UNESCO) entitied and reasonably well placed to act and to offer leadership in this field.[94] On the positive front the declarations tried to protect human dignity through the elaboration of various principles. The reference to human dignity in the two aforementioned international instruments is impressive enough that dignity is sometimes referred to in the literature as "the shaping principle" of international bioethics Nevertheless, it should be recognized that dignity alone is unable to provide a concrete solution to most challenges raised by scientific advances. "Dignity" is not a magic word that can simply be invoked to solve bioethical dilemmas.[95] Further both these declarations does not try to focus on the special needs and concerns of women .Right of access to genetic services, Right to informed Consent, and Confidentiality etc have been talked about in a gender neutral manner.

Indian Legislative Framework

Our is one of the few Constitution which guarantees special rights for women.[96] These guaranteed fundamental rights protect women from violation of fundamental right by the state. Regarding genetic revolution and the ensuing consequences constitution does not explicitly prescribe provisions and safeguards. Article 21which guarantees Right to life can be interpreted to include right to privacy. The Supreme Court in *People's Union for Civil Liberties (PUCL) v. Union of India* [97] held that, the right to privacy is a part of right to "life" and "personal liberty" enshrined under Article 21 of the Constitution, and it cannot be curtailed except according to the procedure established by law. Supreme court has ruled that Medical privacy is not absolute and can be violated for compelling reasons and [98] for prevention of crime, disorder or protection of health or morals or protection of rights and freedom of others. It was held that, having regard to the fact that the appellant was found to be HIV (+), its disclosure would not be violative of either the rule of confidentiality or the appellant's right of privacy as "A", whom the appellant was likely to marry, was saved in time by the disclosure, otherwise, she too would have been infected with the dreadful disease if the marriage had taken place and consummated. If we go by the trend of these decisions it is very clear that though there is not even a single case decided till now directly touching upon the issue of genetic privacy. Indian society is socially very close knit one and one of the problems which will surround the judiciary and policy makers will be to decide whether genetic privacy is individual or familial since the genetic traits are shared among family and generations.

The only regulation in the field of Genetics came through the Guidelines framed by The Department of Bio Technology and The guidelines laid down by ICMR. The ethical committee of Dept of Bio Technology was mandated to deliberate on various issues concerning ethical aspects of the human genome. The efforts and deliberations of the committee resulted in framing Ethical Guidelines for Biomedical Research on Human Subjects. [99]

Throughout the policy document the ethical standard a researcher has to follow has been given lot of significance. The major ethical principles underlined by the document includes

- **Autonomy:** Choice of participation is autonomous, voluntary and based on informed consent; persons or groups with diminished autonomy should be given protection.
- **Privacy:** Identifiable information (clinical, genetic, etc.)

of individuals or groups is confidential and should be protected.

- **Justice:** There should be no discrimination against individuals (born or unborn including embryo) or groups. No harm should be done and benefits should be maximized.
- **Equity:** There should be equitable access to information, tests and procedures.[100]

Realizing the ethical challenges faced by the researchers and medical professional's ICMR came out with ethical guidelines for biomedical research on Human subjects.[101]The principle of informed consent runs along the guidelines it obligates the investigator to obtain the informed consent of the prospective subject. If an individual is not capable of giving informed consent, the consent of legal guardian must be obtained. In case of children, the consent should be obtained from child's parent or legal guardian. Some children, who have not reached the legally established age of consent, but are able to understand the nature of investigation, can give their agreement to serve as research subjects. This agreement is known as 'Assent'. In older children, the consent should be supplemented by assent. The consent can be waived only in exceptional cases.

Further the investigator is obliged to safeguard the confidentiality of research data, which might lead to the identification of the individual participants. Data of individual participants can be disclosed only under certain circumstances like.

- only in a court of law under the orders of the presiding judge or
- there is threat to a person's life or
- in cases of severe adverse reaction may be required to communicate to drug registration authority or

- If there is risk to public health it takes precedence over personal right to privacy and may have to be communicated to health authority.[102]

The council, however, lacks statutory power to ensure that they are being implemented. There are several instances where ethical norms in research in India have been clearly flouted. In a country like India where the even the sex of the foetus can be misused., where organs are sold for a price to where the pressure to survive among the poor can predominate over all ethical values of concern to the western nation, The problem has to be handled at a totally different level and dimension.[103] Adding up to these is the low social and economic status of women. It should be noted that both these declarations elaborates the basic bioethical principles in Gender neutral terms and fails to take into account the special status and requirements of women.

Conclusion

The influence of genetics in medicine is growing and will continue to grow. While it carries with it much promise for improving the prevention and treatment of diseases, there are potential obstacles and repercussions that may hamper this vision. The special problems faced by women are highlighted here. We have a unique opportunity to recommend ways of safeguarding the right of women's before a negative incident happens, and we should seize this chance. After all, prevention is the best cure.

The emerging global consensus on bioethics is clearly minimalist. When addressing the sensitive issue of HGP and women's confidentiality issues, international instruments do not pretend to provide a precise and definitive answer to the most intricate questions posed by medicine and genetics. On the contrary, international bodies tend to lay down very general gender neutral principles like the requirement of informed consent, the confidentiality of health information, the principle of non-discrimination for genetic reasons and the promotion of equity in the allocation of resources in health care, especially to meet the needs of the most disadvantaged populations including women. Though the importance of setting general principles relating to biomedicine should not be understated. It should not be forgotten that national governments, not international organizations, are the primary agents for the realization of human rights.[104]

Regarding the confidentiality of genetic information While the needs and rights of the patient, his or her family members, and the society at large must all be considered when crafting such policies, this chapter argues that, unless the individual is a minor child,[105] a women must have complete control over the uses to which this information is put and to whom it is disseminated. This control should be exercised through the process of informed consent, which includes genetic counseling, pursuant to which the patient is fully advised of the nature of the genetic test, its limitations, the implications for family members, and her right to protect the confidentiality of the information.

References

1 Roberto Andorno, "Biomedicine and International Human Rights Law: in Search of a Global Consensus, "Bulletin of the World Health Organization, 80:959-963, 2002.

2 Oak Ridge Nat'l Laboratory, Human Genome Project Information, Gene Testing, available at http://www.ornl.gov/hgmis/medicine/genetest.html(last visited Dec. 18, 2008).

3 Id.

4 William. S. Klug & Michael. R. Cummings, "Concepts Of Genetics" Prentice Hall 46, 6th ed. 2000).

5 Id.

6 Lawrence M. Fisher, "The Race to Cash in on the Genetic Code," N.Y. TIMES, Aug. 29, 1999, at 3-1.

7 Green Facts Glossary, available at <http://www.greenfacts.org/glossary/def/dna.htm> last visited on 3-04-2009.

8 Id.

9 "Human Genome: The Book of Life" Science, Volume 3 No.5, September-November 2000.

10 Genomics GTL Microbial Genome Project, Human Genome Project Completion, available at http://www.ornl.gov/sci/techresources/Human_Genome/project/50yr.shtml (last visited Jan. 3, 2009).

11 Id.

12 <http://www.ornl.gov/sci/techresourc es/Human_Genome/project/about.html> the site is maintained by U.S. Department of Energy Office of Science, Office of Biological and Environmental Research, Human Genome Program(Last visited on 12-1-2009).

13 Id.

14 Sanger, F., Nicklen, S. and Coulson, A. R., Proc. Natl. Acad. Sci. USA, 74, 5463–5467,1977.

15 Sinsheimer, R. L., Genomics, 5, 954–956, 1985.

16 Summary Report of the Santa Fe Workshop, US Department of Energy, Office of Health and Environmental Research, 3–4 March 1986.

17 Collins, F. S., Patrinos, A., Jordan, E., Chakravarti, A., Gesteland, R. and Walters, L., Science, 282, 682– 689,1988.

18 Id.

19 Dunham, "The DNA Sequence of Human Chromosome 22", Nature 402, at 489, (1999).

20 Declan Butler, "Publication of Human Genomes Sparks Fresh Sequence Debate", Nature 409, at 747-748, 15 February (2000).

21 The Human Genome Project, Hand Book, Genetics Home Reference available at http://ghr.nlm.nih.gov/handbook/hgp Last visited on 4-05-2009.

22 William .R.Rowley, "Biotechnology Overview: Applications and Forecasts" Vol 4 p 4-13,2002.

23 Genomics and Its Impact on Science and Society: The Human Genome Project and Beyond, available at <http://ornl.gov/sci/techresources/Human_Genome/publicat/primer2001/7.shtml>Last visited on 5-06-2009.

24 Id.

25 George .J. Annas, "Mapping the Human Genome Project and the Meaning of Monster Mythology", 39 EmoryL.J.639, (2001).

26 Ibid.

27 Cox SM, Faucett WA, Chen B, Dequeker E, Boone DJ, McGovern MM

"International Genetic Testing." Genetic Med 2003 May;5(3):176-82.

28 Supra note 2.

29 Understanding genetic testing available at http://www.genetech.co.in/downloads/genetic-testing.pdf last visited on 5-04-2009.

30 Id.

31 http://ghr.nlm.nih.gov/handbook/testing/uses Last visited on 4-04-2009.

32 Genetic Testing, Issue brief, Prepared by North Carolina Association for Bio Medical research.

33 Id.

34 Ethical Legal and Social Aspects of Genetic Testing :Research Development and Clinical Applications, The Independent Expert Group, Science and Society, European Commission, 2002.

35 J. C. Goebel, "Prenatal diagnosis of the Rhesus D fetal blood type on amniotic fluid in daily practice" Archives of Gynecology and Obstetrics, Volume 277, p 155-160, 2008.

36 Sudha Kohli, Renu Saxena, Elizabeth Thomas, Pradeep Rao & I.C.Verma, "Prenatal diagnosis of phenylketonuria" Indian J Med Res 122, p 400-403, November 2005.

37 "The Human Genome Project: how do we protect Australians?", The medical Journal of Australia MJA, 173: 596-598, 2000 available at <http://www.mja.com.au/public/issues/173_11_041200/stottdespoja/stottdespoja.html> Last visite don 4-05-2009.

38 Nuffield Council on Bio Ethics, Report on Genetic Screening: Ethical Issues, 1993.

39 Id.

40 Consent and Confidentiality in genetic practice, Guidance on genetic testing and sharing genetic information A report of the Joint Committee on Medical Genetics, 2006.

41 Gerald Dworkin, The Theory and Practice of Autonomy 5-6 (1988).

42 Id.

43 Ian S Markham,"Ethical and Legal Issues," British Medical Bulletin ;54 (No. 4): 1011-1021,1998.

44 Murray TH, Botkin JR. "Genetic Testing and Screening: Ethical Issues. In: Reich WT. (ed) Encyclopaedia of Bioethics, 2nd edn. New York: Macmillan, 1005-10,1995.

45 Callahan D. 'The genetic revolution'. In: Birth and Death; Science and Bioethics. Thomasma D, Kushner T. (eds) Cambridge University Press, 13-20,1996.

46 "Nova Online, Hippocratic Oath—Modern Version, http://www.pbs.org/wgbh/nova/doctors/oath_modern.html (last visited Feb. 15, 2009). This version of the Hippocratic Oath is recited today by many graduating medical schools.

47 Michelle R. King, "Physician Duty to Warn a Patient's Offspring of Hereditary Genetic Defects: Balancing the Patient's Right to Confidentiality Against the Family Member's Right to Know—Can or Should Tarasoff Apply, "4 QUINNIPIAC HEALTH L.J. 1, 5-6 (2000).

48 The Preamble to the Code of Ethics of American Medical association contains the rule it is adopted by the AMA's House of Delegates June 17, 2001. besides this the duties of physicians consist of A physician shall be dedicated to providing competent medical care, with compassion and respect for human dignity and rights., A physician shall uphold the standards of professionalism, be honest in all professional interactions, and strive to report physicians deficient in character or competence, or engaging in fraud or deception, to appropriate entities. A physician shall respect the law and also recognize a responsibility to seek changes in those requirements which are contrary to the best interests of the patient.

49 Martin Richards, "Families, Kinship and Genetics", in The Troubled Helix: Social and Psychological Implications of the New Human Genetics, Martin Richards & Theresa Marteau eds 249-73 , (1996).

50 Id, p 253.

51 Supra note 38 See Nuffield Council.

52 Stewart A. Laidlaw et al., "Genetic Testing and Human Subjects in Research", 24 WHITTIER L. REV. 454, 460 (2002).

53 Id.

54 Id.

55 Susan Nayfield ,, "Potential Role of Tamoxifen in Prevention of Breast Cancer," 83 J. Nat'l Cancer Inst. 1450 (1991).

56 For example, in Hague v. Williams, 181 A.2d 345, 349 (N.J. 1963) it was stated: "[A]lthough ordinarily a physician receives information relating to a patient's health in a confidential capacity ... where the public interest or the private interest of the patient so demands ... disclosure may, under ... compelling circumstances, be made to a person with a legitimate interest in the patient's health."

57 Women and HIV Testing: Policies, Practices, and the Impact on Health and Human Rights, Public health fact Sheet available at http://www.soros.org/initiatives/health/focus/law/articles_publications/publications/womenhiv_20080730/womenhiv_20080730.pdf last visited on 4-05-2009.

58 Id.

59 Horne, 287 So. 2d at 826.

60 551 P.2d 334 (Cal. 1976).

61 614 P.2d 728 (Cal. 1980).

62 Id.

63 Id.

64 432 A.2d. 834 (N.J. 1981).

65 Id. at 838-39.

66 Id. at 836.

67 Supra note 48.

68 American Society of Human Genetics Social Issues Subcommittee on Familial Disclosure, ASHG Statement: Professional Disclosure of Familial Genetic Information, 62 Am. J. Hum. Genet. 474, 483 (1998).

69 Id.

70 NSGC Position Statement: Confidentiality of Test Results (revised 2002), available at <http://www.nsgc.org/about/position.cfm# Confidentiality> (last visited Feb. 15, 2009).

71 Universal Declaration of Human Rights, G.A. Res. 217A (III), U.N. GAOR, 3d Sess., at 71, U.N. Doc. A/810, 1948.

72 International Covenant on Civil and Political Rights, G.A. res. 2200A (XXI), 21 U.N. GAOR Supp. (No. 16) at 52, U.N. Doc. A/6316, 1966.

73 (G.A. res. 2200A (XXI), 21 U.N.GAOR Supp (No. 16) at 49, U.N. Doc. A/6316 (1966), 993 .N.T.S. 3, entered into force Jan. 3, 1976.

74 Supra note71, Art 27(1).

75 Ibid., at Art 7.

76 Id., at Art 25.

77 Supra note 73, Art 15.

78 Id., at Art 12(2).

79 Supra note 72, at Art 7.

80 Ethics and Research On Human Subjects: International Guide lines: Proceedings of The XXVith CIOMAS Conference, Geneva, Switzerland, Feb. 5-7 1992.

81 Final Act of the International Conference on Human Rights, Teheran, 22 April to 13 May 1968, U.N. Doc. A/CONF.32/41.

82 G.A. Res. 152, U.N. GAOR, 53d Sess., U.N. Doc. A/53/625/Add.2 (1998) (hereinafter U.N. General Assembly Resolution on the Human Genome Declaration) (adopting Universal Declaration on the Human

Genome and Human Rights, available online at <http://www.unesco.org/ibc/uk/genome/projet/index.html> (Last on 20-04-2009).

83 European Convention on Human Rights and Biomedicine, Apr. 4, 1997, CETS No. 164, available at http:// conventions.coe.int/treaty/en/treaties/html/164.htm (last visited 3-07-2008) [hereinafter EU Convention]. Thirty-two countries are signatories to the convention. The European Convention on Human Rights and Biomedicine has been ratified, as of January 1, 1999, by Greece, San Marino, Slovakia, and Slovenia. This convention will only enter into force, however, "on the first day of the month following the expiration of a period of three months after the date on which five States, including at least four member States of the Council of Europe, have expressed their consent to be bound by the Convention . . . ." European Convention on Human Rights and Biomedicine.

84 Art. 15.1(b) of (Assisted Human Reproduction) (B.O.E., 1988, 282) (authorizing research on human embryos up to 14 days of development) (hereinafter Spanish Law of 1988 on Assisted Human Reproduction); Art. 2(e) of (Donation and Use of Human Embryos and Fetuses, or Their Cells, Tissues and Organs) (B.O.E., 1988, 314) (permitting donation and use of embryos for research or experimental purposes only of "clinically unviable or dead" embryos and fetuses). (Fetus Protection Act), v. 13.12.1990 (BGBl. I S.2746).

86 Human Fertilisation and Embryology Act, 1990, ch. 37, § 3 (U.K.).

87 Access to Medical Reports Act 1988.

88 Supra note 82 Art 12(b).

89 Id Art 5 (a).

90 Id Art 5(c) The right of each individual to decide whether or not to be informed of the results of genetic examination and the resulting consequences should be respected.

91 Id Art 9.

92 Supra note 83 Art 5.

93 Id Art 10.

94 UNESCO - the United Nations Educational, Scientific and Cultural Organization (UNESCO) was founded on 16 November 1945. Its stated purpose is to contribute to peace and security by promoting international collaboration through education, science, and culture in order to further universal respect for justice, the rule of law, and the human rights and fundamental freedoms proclaimed in the UN Charter.

95 Supra note 1 See Roberto.

96 Constitution of India Art 15(3).

97 1997, 1 SCC 301.

98 Mr."X" v. Hospital "Z", 1998, 8 SCC 296.

99 Ethical Policies on the Human Genome, Genetic Research & Services, by Department of Bio technology available at <http://dbtindia.nic.in/institutions/instmain.html> (last visited on 23-09-2007).

100 Ibid.

101 Ethical Guidelines for Biomedical Research on Human Subjects by ICMR available at http://www.icmr.nic.in/ethical_guidelines.pdf (last visited on 5-11-2008).

102 Ibid.

103 G.Padmanabhan, "Gene therapy "in Human Genome Research, Emerging Ethical Legal Social and Economic Issues edt MG.K Menon and others, at 114, (2003).

104 Supra note 1 see Robert.

105 Roger B. Dworkin, "Getting What We Should from Doctors: Rethinking Patient Autonomy and the Doctor-Patient Relationship" 13 Health Matrix 235 (2003).

3

Stem Cell Research, Impact on Health and Dignity of Women: A Legal and Ethical Analysis

Introduction

In November of 1998, James Thomson and John Gearhart announced their respective successes in deriving human embryonic stem cells (hESCs) and human germ stem cells. Many in the scientific community greeted this news with considerable enthusiasm.[1] Others, however, including some members of the scientific community, were much less optimistic; some expressed concern about the moral status of embryos and fetuses, and others expressed concern about the risks to women and couples who would provide the embryos and fetal tissue for research use.[2] These and other ethical concerns have since been the subject of intense international debate not only in the media and academia, but also in numerous governmental and quasi-governmental reports.[3] Women's health and human rights advocates throughout the world are increasingly concerned that overzealous pursuit of new scientific discoveries may once again be threatening women's health. The chapter critically analyzes the ethical and legal issues rising out of Stem cell research in relation to women rights. Chapter explore the legislative and judicial response in this field with special reference to India.

Stem Cell: Conceptual Dimensions

The human body is an elaborate mass of cells, each with a defined role and organised into tissues and organs. Every cell, whether in the liver, heart or brain, takes on its role by specialising into a particular cell type, with a characteristic shape and function, through a process called cell differentiation.[4] Differentiation begins early in embryonic development and eventually leads to over 200 diverse cell types, whose orchestrated activity form the human body. The idea of "stem cells", immature cells from which all specialised cell types derive, emerged in the late nineteenth century in response to fundamental questions in embryology, such as the origin of the blood system.[5] However, due to the limitations of the experimental methods available at the time, stem cells remained largely hypothetical until research on survivors of the 1945 nuclear bombings was carried out and the term re-emerged to describe cellular regeneration mechanisms found to exist throughout the body.[6]

Stem cells are defined by the International Society for SCR (ISSCR) as " Cells that have both the capacity to self-renew and make more stem cells by cell division as well as to differentiate into mature, specialized cells.[7] In 1978, a group of scientists, composed mainly of haematologists, decided upon the following definition for stem cells" Cells with extensive self-maintaining (self-renewal capacity), extending throughout the whole or most of the life-span of the organism. Differentiation potential is a property of some types of stem cells but it is not an essential feature of stem-ness.[8]

Thus stem cells are 'unspecialised' or 'undifferentiated' cells, which means that they are immature cells that have not yet been directed to become a specialized cell with a specific function e.g. a blood pumping heart cell. Stem cells have two unique characteristics:

- The capacity for unlimited or prolonged self-renewal
- The capacity to differentiate into at least one type of differentiated or specialised cell.[9]

Stem cells are regarded by many as the holy grail of medicine. Harold Varmus, former director of the National Institutes of Health (NIH) in the US, said with regard to stem cell research that "there is almost no realm in medicine that might not be touched by this innovation."[10] Different kinds of stem cells can be distinguished according to their potential to differentiate. They are progenitor, multipotent or pluripotent stem cells.

- Progenitor stem cells are those whose terminally differentiated progeny consist of a single cell type only. For instance, epidermal stem cells or spermatogonial stem cells can differentiate respectively into only keratinocytes and spermatozoa.[11]
- Multipotent stemcells are those which can give rise to several terminally differentiated cell types constituting a specific tissue or organ. Examples are skin stem cells which give rise to epidermal cells, sebaceous glands and hair follicles or haematopoietic stem cells, which give rise to all the diverse blood cells and neural stem cells, which give rise to all the cell types in the nervous system, including glia and the many different types of neurons.
- Pluripotent stem cells are able to give rise to all different cell types Pluripotent stem cells, which are isolated from primordial germ cells in the foetus, are called: embryonic germ cells ("EG cells"). Those stem cells, which are isolated from the inner cell mass of a blastocyst-stage embryo, are called embryonic stem cells ("ES cells").[12]

Another way of classifying stem cells is according to the source they were derived from. Stem cells may be derived from fluids and tissues from humans from the moment of conception until after death. On this basis generally, stem cells are classified as adult, fetal or embryonic stem cells. More recently, umbilical cord blood stem cells, sometimes called 'neonatal' stem cells, have been added as a separate category.

Adult stem cells can be found in many tissues and organs in humans after birth throughout their whole life, primarily in the bone marrow, but also in peripheral and cord blood, the brain, spinal cord, gum tissue, epithelia of the skin and digestive system, cornea, retina, liver, teeth and many more. It has usually been assumed that adult stem cells are multipotent, that is, only capable of developing into cell types of the associated organ or area of the body.[13] Adult stem cells have one enormous advantage over stem cells from most other sources they can be harvested from the patient, ruling out the possibility of immune rejection after transplantation. Immune rejection occurs when the recipient's body fails to accept a transplanted tissue or organ because it is recognised as foreign, and consequently attempts to destroy it.[14]

The most versatile type of stem cell is the embryonic stem (ES) cell. ES cells were first isolated in mice in 1981[15] in animals and in humans in 1998.[16] There are two main sources of human embryonic stem cells for research. The majority are obtained from embryos produced, but not used, during *in vitro* fertilisation (IVF) treatment.[17] For many reasons, including the completion of a family or separation from a partner, the embryos made for IVF may not all be used by the couple undergoing treatment. Currently, there are four options for embryos that are not used during IVF treatment: they can be placed in storage, allowed to perish, donated to someone else for IVF treatment, or donated for use in stem cell research.[18] Through the derivation process the embryo is 'dismantled' and impeded in its further development to a human. Some say the embryo is 'killed' or 'destroyed' through the derivation process. Alternatively, embryonic stem cells can be obtained from embryos made by somatic cell nuclear transfer (SCNT), a technique otherwise known as cloning.[19]

The possibility of human cloning, raised when Scottish scientists at Roslin Institute created the much-celebrated sheep 'Dolly', aroused worldwide interest and concern because of its scientific and ethical implications.[20] The feat, also generated uncertainty over the meaning of 'cloning' - an umbrella term traditionally used by scientists to describe different processes for duplicating biological material.

There are different types of cloning and cloning technologies can be used for other purposes besides producing the genetic twin of another organism. A basic understanding of the different types of cloning is key to taking an informed stance on current public policy issues and making the best possible personal decisions. The following three types of cloning technologies exist :

- recombinant DNA technology or DNA cloning,
- reproductive cloning, and
- therapeutic cloning.[21]

Reproductive cloning is a technology used to generate an animal that has the same nuclear DNA as another currently or previously existing animal. Dolly was created by reproductive cloning technology.[22] In a process called 'somatic cell nuclear transfer' Therapeutic cloning, also called 'embryo cloning,' is the production of human embryos for use in research. Cloning carried out for this specific purpose is commonly referred to as therapeutic cloning, because the cloned embryo is made solely to obtain embryonic stem cells for research or therapy. This process carries certain special threat for women which are the focus of this chapter.

Large numbers of cells are needed for stem cell replacement therapies. Due to these one of the main focuses of the discussion has been on the ability of various stem cells to differentiate into a range of cell types, which may be useful in cell therapy. Indeed, stem cells differ considerably in the amount and type of different cells they can become. Embryonic stem cells can be relatively easily grown in culture, They are either totipotent or pluripotent and can give rise to all of the cell types of the body, In 1998, John Gearhart and his team at the Johns Hopkins University School of Medicine was the first to establish this pluripotent stem cells from human fetuses or post-implantation embryos. The embryonic germ (EG) cells thus obtained have been shown to give rise to cell types of the three germ layers, and can thus be called pluripotent. [23]

Whereas adult stem cells are predominantly multipotent, meaning they are generally limited to specializing into the different cell types of their tissue of origin. The distinction between adult and embryonic stem cells is popular for the purposes of the ethical discussion surrounding research involving the destruction of embryos. **(Table 1)**

Difference Between Embryonic and Adult Stem Cells

Embryonic Stem Cells	Adult Stem Cells
They are relatively plentiful and are easier to grow in the laboratory than adult stem cells.	They are present in very small numbers and aredifficult to access. They can also be difficult to grow in the laboratory.
They can develop into any type of cell found in the body	Currently, they are known to develop into a restricted number of different cell types, usually related to the type of tissue they are found in.
They would not be genetically matched to the individual being treated and could possibly be rejected by his or her immune system.	They can be genetically matched to the individual being treated and would not be rejected by his or her immune system.
If not fully differentiated into a cell type with a specialised function, embryonic stem cells can form tumours	There is less evidence to suggest that cells and tissues derived from adult stem cells will develop tumours.

Source :Stem cell Information leaflet , Irish Council on Bio ethics

Benefits

Evaluating the beneficial consequences of embryonic stem cell research is not straightforward. There are complexities associated with assessing how realistic the potential of the benefits. It is believed that recent scientific and technical developments in the field of stem cell research hold great promise of application of this knowledge to human welfare specially medicine. Most attention has centered on the medical potential of stem cell research and cultivation, and the generation of replacement tissues and organs for transplant.[24] Because of their proliferation and differentiation capacities they are widely believed to represent the greatest promise for medicine in the twenty-first century.[25] This includes replacement of cells/tissues lost due to trauma, degeneration or loss of blood supply. The degeneration could be both age related, as well as due to genetic disorders which can occur at any time of life. Further they could be used to treat a variety of diseases and conditions, including diabetes, Parkinson's disease, heart disease, spinal cord injuries, blindness, deafness and many types of cancer. There is also a possibility of developing organs using stem cells seeded on to appropriate scaffoldings. [26] Unlike current drugs, which mainly delay symptoms of diseases, stem cells may make it possible to replace damaged tissue or even whole organs. Their value extends beyond utility in cell therapy. Stem cells are also useful tools for fundamental research, mainly for gaining knowledge about early human development, cell division and differentiation mechanisms, gene and protein function, for developing drugs and toxicity testing, and for developing models of human diseases. [27] This immense promise gives powerful moral reasons for pursuing stem cell research.

Ethical Concerns

Stem cell research raises serious ethical considerations and most of these issues surround the validity of embryonic stem cell research. The reason being embryonic research ultimately, depends on the use of human embryos as a source of stem cells and, consequently, on the destruction of the embryos. A range of positions can be taken with respect to the moral status of embryos. At one end of the spectrum, is the view that embryos are balls of cells that have no more moral value than any other piece of human biological material.[28] At the other end, some would consider embryos to have the same moral status as any adult. This is the view that embryos have "full" moral status from the moment fertilisation is complete.[29] Others grant significant value to early embryos but not the same status as they would grant to an adult. In discussing the moral status of embryos, various commentators refer to what can be called the "potentiality argument".[30] The view is often expressed that embryos are due considerable moral status because they are "part of the human family" or "one of us". Such expressions suggest that, even if embryos do not qualify for personhood, their moral status should be considered in light of their potential to develop into fully fledged persons. These expressions also imply that there is something intrinsically special about human life. Whether destructive embryonic stem cell research is the right thing to do or not, will partly depend on what the alternatives are, and how their particular benefits and drawbacks balance out. There is another research program involving adult stem cells that are present in and drawn from bone marrow, brain and gut, and other tissues. Some of these stem cells have a capacity to differentiate into a limited number of different cell types, such as blood cells, muscles and neurones (i.e., they are multipotent), but they have not been shown to be pluripotent in the way that embryonic stem cells are.[31] This limitation means that adult stem cells offer more limited potential benefits in regenerative medicine and gene therapy, at least from the standpoint of our current understanding and available biotechnology.[32]

Threat to women

In the world discourse on stem cells the debate about cell research has centered on whether human embryos should be used for research. It has left nearly untouched a number of important social, political and ethical issues unrelated to the moral status of embryos. Among the most important are those concerning the health and safety of women who provide eggs for research. One strong but minority strand of argument emphasises the impact that biotechnology has on broader social relationships. It has been argued that 'research should be evaluated not only in terms of its effects on the subjects of the experiment but also in terms of its connection with existing patterns of oppression and domination in society'.[33] There is a considerable body of writing that explores the impacts of new reproductive technologies (such as IVF) on the interests of women, particularly how those technologies might contribute to oppression.[34] In the case of embryonic research, it is sometimes argued that women who donate ova or embryos are at risk of exploitation to the extent that male-dominated medical practice appropriates their reproductive labour for research and commercial benefits. Moreover, it is argued that women's body parts are at risk of being commodified, and their acts of altruistic donation demeaned, if downstream users can develop commercial applications for stem cells developed from their ova and embryos.[35]

Currently, the main source of hES cells are embryos left over from fertility treatment and donated after informed consent by their conceivers. Another possible source is embryos created by IVF with gametes donated solely for research purposes, so-called 'research embryos'. Some scientists are attempting to use another technique, known as research cloning or somatic cell nuclear transfer (SCNT). The nature of human embryos is central to the cloning debate, but so is the welfare of women who would supply human eggs. Yet both supporters and opponents rarely mention this element of cloning. SCNT involves inserting the nucleus of an adult body cell into an egg whose nucleus has been removed. The process requires a large number of women's eggs. In order to procure eggs, researchers typically give women hormonal treatments to first "shut down" and then "hyperstimulate" their ovaries, followed by surgical extraction of multiple eggs. [36] This invasive process can give rise to serious health and other issues.

Health Issues

The harvesting of multiple eggs is an invasive and uncomfortable two-stage process requiring many clinic visits, multiple injections of hormones, and minor surgery at the least. Both stages, ovarian suppression and what is known as 'ovarian stimulation', require the use of powerful hormones and other drugs to manipulate a woman's body into producing many, The drug most often used to shut down the ovaries, Lupron, can cause side effects, including severe joint pain, difficulty breathing, chest pain, depression, amnesia, hypertension, and asthma[37] The most immediate serious risk from ovarian stimulation is ovarian hyperstimulation syndrome (OHSS).[38] The American Society of Reproductive Medicine (ASRM) acknowledges that mild forms of OHSS occur in 10–20% of cycles.[39] Others have published similar estimates.[40] Symptoms of mild forms of OHSS include nausea, vomiting, diarrhoea, and abdominal distention. which in the most severe cases can lead to hospitalization and, rarely, death.[41]The long term risks of ovarian stimulation are poorly understood. As Suzanne Parisian former Chief Medical Officer of the United States Food and Drug Administration (FDA), explains, 'Pharmaceutical firms have not been required by either the government or physicians to collect safety data for IVF drugs regarding risk of cancer or other serious health conditions despite the drugs having been available in the world for several decades.[42]

Beyond direct risks to the women undergoing ovarian stimulation, one must also consider possible effects of exposure to the drugs used on the offspring of treated women. Here, too, human data are sorely lacking. However, a recent report that ovarian stimulation treatment in mice results in several significant abnormalities in their offspring does provide reason for concern. These effects include growth retardation, a delay in ossif cation.[43] It is to be remembered that treatments based on embryonic stem cells and SCNT are still highly experimental. Multiple egg extraction poses risks to women's health without a clear and demonstrable scientific rationale.

Compensation and Comodification : One of the primary issues in the debate is whether women should be paid for their eggs. Paying women will likely be a financial inducement for economically vulnerable women to undergo a process in which the long term effects are not clearly understood. Offering payment beyond direct expenses commercializes reproductive material and creates a market for human eggs, which could lead to the exploitation of economically vulnerable women. [44] Already in the US a woman can be paid as much as USD 80000 to donate her eggs for IVF procedures. Women recruited for their eggs for IVF are often college students who have been selected for their 'top genetic makeup.' But in research cloning it does not matter whom the eggs come from because the nucleus which contains the genetic material of the egg is removed. This means that low income women of are more likely to be targeted for recruitment. We are concerned that a market in women's reproductive tissue will be created in the research context.[45]

However, on the other spectrum it should be noted that, research subjects are often paid for their involvement in drug trials, to compensate them for the time and effort invested in taking part in the research project. Therefore, it has been argued that women should be compensated for their time, travel and inconvenience, as well as for the risks undertaken during the egg harvesting procedure.[46]

Exploitation

The potential for exploitation of young women can be expected to rise with an increasing demand for human eggs created by embryonic stem cell or cloning research, thus complicating an already problematic situation. In a speech of the Holy See to the UN, Archbishop Migliore stated that, "the process of obtaining these eggs, which is not without risk, would use women's bodies as mere reservoirs of oocytes, instrumentalizing women and undermining their dignity".[47] This can be substantiated by the fact that an international market for human eggs emerged in the early 1990s in response to the growth of the IVF industry, and this market has become the most competitive link in the supply chain of what Debora Spar refers to as 'the baby business.[48] The recent cloning scandal involving Korean and American researchers illustrates how investigators' needs could distort, if not corrupt, standard ethical principles and underscores our concerns about risks to women from whom eggs are extracted solely for research. In February 2004, Korean scientist, Hwang Woo-suk claimed to have successfully derived stem cells from a human embryo made by inserting the nucleus of a somatic (body) cell from an adult into the enucleated (nucleus removed) egg cell from an unrelated female.[49] Had these reports been true, they would have constituted a major breakthrough in research cloning, also referred to as somatic cell nuclear transfer (SCNT). Initial reports indicated that Hwang's team required 242 human eggs to create one embryo. Then in 2005, he claimed to have generated '11 patient-specific stem-cell lines with a success rate of one line for approximately every 20 oocytes'.[50] This seemed to suggest a significant reduction in the number of eggs required to create one clone, and fuelled much media attention to the possible 'cures' of a range of chronic diseases. However, later it was shown not only were the reported research results fraudulent, but also Hwang used well over 2000 eggs without ever creating a viable human clonal embryo. Furthermore, it has been revealed that payment, coercion and lying were used to acquire the eggs first reported to have been eagerly donated by participating women.[51]

With the threat of health hazards and exploitation there are experts who believe that women participating in cloning studies must be considered research subjects entitled to the same rights and protections as other people undergoing potentially harmful procedures for the sake of advancing science. Women in cloning research receive drugs to make them produce many more eggs than usual. They undergo a few weeks of injections, sedation for egg retrieval and a series of tests and clinic visits. Besides triggering menopause-like symptoms, the drugs expose women to a small chance of serious health problems and a remote risk of death. No clear long-term risks have been documented, but some experts worry about an increased possibility of cancer or infertility. They believe that women must understand these risks before choosing to help with research cloning.[52]

It can be argued that, if sufficient safeguards are in place like research ethics review, counseling sessions and once fully informed, women should be allowed to voluntarily donate their eggs for research as an expression of their personal autonomy. If a woman has given such consent it may be inappropriate to consider her as being instrumentalised. In this respect, the accuracy and extent of the information provided as part of the consent process is vital. Prohibiting women from undertaking the risks inherent in egg donation could be considered to be overly paternalistic and inconsistent with practice in other areas of research. Reasonable limits to financial compensation, registration of all donors and limiting the number of cycles for donation may represent a possible means of addressing concerns relating to exploitation.[53]

The UN Declaration on Human Cloning also stresses this point and calls upon Member States to take measures to prevent the exploitation of women in the application of life sciences. However, the problem of the need for large numbers of eggs from women is likely to be a short term problem for several reasons. First, one of the main purposes of cloning is to perform research to understand how cells develop and can be programmed to an immature state. Once that is understood, the process can be replicated in a laboratory and there will be no need for new eggs. Second, researchers are investigating the use of alternatives, including fetal oocytes and eggs from adult ovaries, obtained post mortem or during operation.[54] In June 2005, a team of Belgian scientists reported at the annual conference of the European Society of Human Reproduction and Embryology (ESHRE) that they had cloned human embryos using human eggs matured in the laboratory.[55] They hope one day this will make it possible to perform therapeutic cloning by creating artificial eggs from patients' body cells. Another alternative is the differentiation of ES cells in culture into germ cells and full-grown oocytes.[56] Once these technologies are perfected women will not be required to donate large number of eggs.

International Legal Position

Given the promise offered by the emerging dimensions of stem cell technology, it has become incumbent to regulate the same and converge the interests of the scientific community, healthcare professionals and patients. In fact, policy makers in most parts of the globes have been grappling with the ethical questions that the onset of stem cell technology presents. What we witness is a pieced together inconsistent regulations and recommended guidelines addressing SCNT and egg extraction.

At the national level many countries have enacted some form of regulations or legislations relating to stem cell research and these regulations ranges from complete opposition to complete permission. Sweden and the Netherlands are generally regarded as having the most "liberal" rules. In December 2001, the Swedish Research Council issued guidelines endorsing the use of CNR but not of the creation of embryos by IVF for research) subject to certain conditions, including legislation to prohibit placing such embryos in a woman. [57] Britain also comes across as an enthusiastic supporter of ES cell research, It amended its law to allow ES cells to be isolated from human blastocysts – the hollow ball of cells that form after some five days of embryological development – for research into regenerative medicine.[58] Japan has also prepared guidelines that will give its researchers similar freedom. Israel and Australia are also supportive of work on human ES cells. In Italy, the law on assisted reproduction prohibits hES cell research perhaps due to the strong influence of Vatican on Italy's policymaking. [59] The same goes with Ireland's legislation as well. Ireland is the only European country that defends "the right to life of the unborn" in its constitution.[60] hES cell research is strictly forbidden, as is the case in Austria[61] and Norway.[62] Costa Rica, Brazil and Ecuador ban hES cell research. Only a minority of countries worldwide strictly prohibit research on hES cell cells.

At the regional level a pan-European initiative saw the formation of the Group of Advisers on the Ethical Implications of Biotechnology (GAEIB) to the EC in 1991. The GAEIB was established to examine the ethical questions associated with biotechnology. In May 1997, the GAEIB produced an opinion document entitled Ethical Aspects of Cloning Techniques, which made a number of recommendations concerning cloning research involving humans and animals.[63] This document recommended that human reproductive cloning should be prohibited and that any research involving nuclear substitution (SCNT) in human embryos should be conducted to help overcome disease and alleviate suffering.[64]

It is to be understood that most of these national and international instruments in this field are concerned with reproductive cloning rather than research on human embryos.[65] But at the Regional level the European Convention on Human Rights and Biomedicine makes a number of references to research involving embryos and cloning.[66] Article 18.1 of the Convention permits research on embryos in vitro where the

National legislation allows, provided the embryos are afforded sufficient protection. [67]Article 18.2 expressly forbids the creation of human embryos for research purposes.[68] As of March 2009, 34 Member States of the Council of Europe have signed the Convention, and 21 of these have ratified it. The Convention is only binding in Member States that have ratified it.

At the global level United Nations came up with a declaration on Cloning.[69] It called upon the member states to prohibit all forms of human cloning in as much as they are incompatible with human dignity and the protection of human life; and adopt measures necessary to protect adequately human life in the application of life sciences. It also emphasized that the promotion of scientific and technical progress in life sciences should be sought in a manner that safeguards respect for human rights and the benefit of all. The note worthy aspect of the declaration is the specific concern for women. Declaration enjoins the Member States take measures to prevent the exploitation of women in the application of life sciences. Preamble to the declaration also highlights the rights of women. Preamble recognizes serious medical, physical, psychological and social dangers that human cloning may imply for the individuals involved, and also conscious of the need to prevent the exploitation of women.[70]

An analysis of most of these legislations and regulations prove that there are no adequate policies or legislative safeguards for women who provide their eggs for stem cell research. Most regulations either permitted or banned the therapeutic cloning based on its policy or attitude in relation to the legal and moral status of embryo. Regulations almost ignored or failed to look into the specific threat women faces in the wake of therapeutic cloning. For this reason there is a lack of oversight of research and a lack of accountability on the part of researchers. For instance USA the pioneer in the stem cell research lacks legislations which takes into account gender concerns. There are voluntary guidelines issued by the

US National Research Council and Institute of Medicine of the National Academies, and two states California and Massachusetts) have some type of regulation. California's law is the most comprehensive regarding egg retrieval for research, and includes provisions to safeguard women's health and prevent commodification.[71] It ensures that women be given medically accurate information about the risks of egg retrieval, mandates that any woman who experiences adverse reactions from the procedure and needs medical treatment will not have to pay for it herself, and sets rules for disclosure of conflicts of interest between the medical personnel who conduct the egg retrieval procedures and the researchers working on cloning techniques.[72] The aspect of the law that has drawn most attention is the limit it places on paying women for providing eggs for research. In order to head off the emergence of a market in eggs for research, the law limits payment to reimbursement for direct expenses. If payments were permitted, researchers would likely be offering thousands of dollars to recruit women to supply eggs, encouraging their acceptance of known short-term health risks, and long-term risks that are little understood.[73] Canada has some amount a more comprehensive legislation. In Canada, women's health is more central both to the debate around stem cell research and to policy.[74]

In the absence of specific gender concerns in legislation, many point to the concept of human dignity. Human dignity is often appealed to in bioethics and has been widely integrated into human rights documents. Indeed, the concept of human dignity runs through the length and breadth of all human right doctrines.[75] Further Article 1 of the Charter of Fundamental Rights of the European Union states that, "Human dignity is inviolable."[76] According to Immanuel Kant, who brought the concept of human dignity to the fore in western philosophical thought, human beings have incomparable value because they are moral agents who are responsible for their own actions.[77]

A major difficulty with the notion of human dignity is that it is often employed to justify both sides of a particular debate, which indicates that its exact meaning is elusive. This has been appropriately captured by Adam Schulman's introduction to a working paper submitted to the President's Council on Bioethics in the US: Human dignity—is it a useful concept in bioethics, one that sheds important light on the whole range of bioethical issues, from embryo research and assisted reproduction, to biomedical enhancement, to care of the disabled and the dying? Or is it, on the contrary, a useless concept—at best a vague substitute for other, more precise notions, at worst a mere slogan that camouflages unconvincing arguments and unarticulated biases?[78] Thus it is imperative in the interest of humanity that regulations on stem cell address the specific gender concerns rather than leaving it to be determined by the vague concept of 'dignity'.

Indian Legislative Approach

The stem cell research holds great promise of improving human health by control of degenerative diseases and restoration of damage to organs by various injuries[79] India is no exception.

Leaving aside some scattered provisions in the Constitution, India does not have any specific legislation on the impact of science and technology on Human Rights and women. With regard to stem cells Indian Council of Medical Research (ICMR) have come up with certain guidelines.[80] The guidelines have taken into consideration both potential risks of basic and clinical research in this field, as well as potential benefits of stem cell knowledge to human well being, to arrive at a regulatory framework for stem cell research and therapy that is not too restrictive for research. The guidelines categorise stem cells into three categories on the basis of their origin.

- Human embryonic stem (hES) cells, derived from the blastocysts: which are derived from various sources including surplus embryos from IVF clinics, created specifically for research using IVF, created by techniques like SCNT etc.[81]

- Human embryonic germ (hEG) cells, which are derived from primordial germ cells of the fetus.[82]
- Human somatic stem (hSS) cells, which are derived from fetal or adult tissues or organs, including umbilical cord blood / placenta.[83]

The most salient aspect of these guidelines is the categorization of stem cell studies into three groups, including permissive, restrictive and prohibitive research;[84] and to suggest a provision for two tiers of evaluation, one at the institutional level for permissive research and the other at the national level for restrictive research. For example, reproductive cloning being repugnant to the society has been put in the prohibitive category. Another clear area of prohibited research is *in vitro* culture or manipulation of human embryo beyond 14 days after fertilization, or formation of neural tube, whichever occurs earlier. [85]

For implementation and monitoring of the Guidelines for Stem Cell Research and Therapy two separate Institutional, and National Stem Cell Research and Therapy Committees are proposed.[86] This independent mechanism has been proposed considering highly specialized nature of stem cell research and to assure compliance with the laid down responsibilities of the investigator and the institution involved with stem cell research. One of the important functions of the Institutional SCRT Committee will be to decide whether the research falls in the permissive, restrictive or prohibited categories.[87] This would require special expertise, hence the need for a separate committee. The Institutional SCRT will also be responsible to ensure that the National Guidelines for Stem Cell Research and Therapy are complied which can be reviewed after a few years of operationalization.[88] It has to be noted that the Institutional

SCRT Committee, besides evaluating the proposals on research in restricted areas shall also serve as a policy laying down body, which would periodically review the National Guidelines in light of new developments in the field. The national Apex Committee shall serve to register all the stem cell research centers in the country, available stem cell lines in the country, including the newly developed ones, and ongoing clinical stem cell trials in the country. The function of the National Committee will also be to receive periodic reports from the Institutional SCRTs and to provide status of SCRT in the country from time to time.[89]

A distinction has also been made between establishing embryonic stem cell lines from spare embryos and embryos specifically made for the purpose, including both in vitro fertilization and somatic cell nuclear transfer techniques. The former is kept in the permissive category provided spare embryos are obtained in an ethically acceptable manner while later is kept in the restrictive category to require specific scientific justification and proof of technical competence of the investigator.[90] It has been done to dissuade frivolous creation of embryos for establishment of hES cell lines. In this context detailed guidelines have also been developed regarding procurement of gametes, blastocysts or somatic cells for generation of hES cell lines.[91] Special guidelines have been made regarding precautions to be taken while using umbilical cord blood stem cells (and foetal stem cells) for research and therapy since foetus or the newborn cannot be the consenting partner. The basic principles include safety of the mother and the newborn, quality assurance of the product, and provision of appropriate and correct information to parents while taking their consent for collection of the cells/tissues. This is particularly important since umbilical cord stem cell banks are mushrooming both in the public and private sectors. The guidelines permit all proposals involving fetuses or fetal tissue, for research or therapy except termination of pregnancy with a view to donate fetal tissue in return for possible financial or therapeutic benefits. Further the guidelines lays down that consent to have a termination of pregnancy and the donation of fetal material for purpose of research or therapy should be taken separately, the medical person responsible for the care of the pregnant woman planning to undergo termination of pregnancy and the person who will be using the fetal material should not be the same, the women shall not have the option to specify the use for a particular person or in a particular way and the identity of the donor and the recipient should be kept confidential.[92]

In relation to therapeutic cloning and the interests of women the guidelines provides that women who undergo hormonal induction to generate oocytes specifically for research purposes (such as for SCNT) may be reimbursed for direct expenses incurred as a result of the procedure, as determined by the IC-SCRT/ IEC. Further they should be informed about potential hazards, complications etc which are related to the hormonal induction process. [93] The attending physician responsible for the infertility treatment and the investigator deriving or proposing to use hES cells preferably should not be the same person. To facilitate autonomous choice, decisions related to the creation of embryos for infertility treatment should be free of the influence of investigators who propose to derive or use hES cells in research.[94]

These guidelines provide a mechanism to ensure that a research with human stem cells is conducted in a responsible and ethically sensitive manner and complies with all regulatory requirements pertaining to biomedical research in general and stem cell research in particular.[95] At the same time it is to be seen that enough attention has not been given to the special concerns of women undergoing SCNT process.

Conclusion

"Every truly effective technological advance is a challenge to culture, politics and ethics. This is as true for discoveries of fire, the wheel and gunpowder, as it is for the Atom bomb, space travel and biotechnology", said Edmund Pellegrino of the Georgetown University Medical Center and new Chair of the US President's Council on Bioethics.[96] Indeed, like many new technologies stem cell research raises several substantial ethical issues and creates a challenge for all societies.

Till now the debate about stem cells have more or less centered around the moral and legal status of embryo. Focusing on one particular view on the moral status of embryos may crystallise various issues in this crucial contemporary debate. But we risk neglecting other issues that may be important to the problem, If we really do care about human lives, then we should not continue to be hostages of one particular viewpoint on the moral status of the embryo, but we should start to focus on other issues including gender concerns.

It is imperative that law on stem cell explicitly addresses the concern of women. In the absence of legislations certain guidelines are prescribed for researchers

- Researchers should be required to adopt the safest and most ethical approaches to procuring eggs for SCNT. [97]
- Researchers should investigate alternatives to hormonally-stimulated egg retrieval.
- Provide accurate and complete information
- Researchers must try to reduce women's exposure to harm.
- More extensive data on the health effects of egg extraction needs to be gathered, and should be reviewed by an independent oversight body.
- Egg extraction should be conducted by physicians who have no financial conflicts of interest with the research for which the eggs will be used.
- Women who provide eggs for research should be reimbursed only for direct expenses, in order to prevent

the creation of a market in eggs. This is the view taken by the Californian Law

- Researchers or their funding agencies should cover medical costs of treating adverse reactions associated with egg extraction procedures.
- Regulatory bodies with authority to enforce the above standards should be established.[98]

Further scientists and researchers can take assistance from the ethical guidelines of the American Society for Reproductive Medicine, which were prepared for infertility clinics. [99]According to the guidelines, women providing eggs to others should be cared for by doctors whose primary concern is the donors' health, not the success of egg retrieval. These doctors first should concentrate on whether women are healthy enough to begin and complete the donation process. Women must be free to withdraw for medical or other reasons.[100]

References

1 Elliott Marshall, "A Versatile Cell Line Raises Scientific Hopes, Legal Questions" 282 Science 1014 (1988). and Davor Solter & John Gearhart, "Putting Stem Cells to Work" 283 Science 1468, (1999).

2 Suzanne Holland "Beyond the Embryo: A Feminist Appraisal of the Embryonic Stem Cell Debate" in Suzanne Holland, Karen Lebacqz & Laurie Zoloth, eds., The Human Embryonic Stem Cell Debate: Science, Ethics, and Public Policy Cambridge, MIT Press,p 73 (2001) Ingrid Schneider & Claudia Schumann, "Stem Cells, Therapeutic Cloning, Embryo Research: Women as Raw Material Suppliers for Science and Industry" Proceedings of ReproKult: Women's Forum for Reproductive Medicine; Reproductive Medicine and Genetic Engineering; Women Between Self-Determination and Societal Standardisation, Berlin, 15 - 17 November 2001 79, online: ReproKult <http://www.reprokult.de/e_forum_3.pdf>. Last visited on 3-05-2009.

3 Audrey R. Chapman, Mark S. Frankel & Michele S. Garfinkle, Stem Cell Research and Applications: Monitoring the Frontiers of Biomedical Research, American Association for the Advancement of Science & Institute for Civil Society, Washington, D.C., (1999), online: <http://www.aaas.org/spp/sfrl/projects/stem/report.pdf>;Last visited on 4-5-2009 U.K., Department of Health, Government Response to the

Recommendations Made in the Chief Medical Officer's Expert Group Report "Stem Cell Research: Medical Progress with Responsibility" by Secretary of State for Health (2000), online: http://www.dh.gov.uk/ assetRoot/ 04/05/77/34/04057734.pdfLast visited on 4-05-2009 Australian Academy of Science, On Human Cloning: A Position Statement (Cranberra: Australian Academy of Science, 1999), online: http://www.science.org.au/reports/clone.pdf Last visited on 5-05-2009. U.S., National Bioethics Advisory Commission, Ethical Issues in Human Stem Cell Research: Report and Recommendations of the National Bioethics Advisory Commission, (Rockville, MD: National Bioethics Advisory Commission, 1999), online: <http:// www.bioethics.gov/reports/past_commissions/ nbac_stemcell1.pdf> Lastvisited on 5-04-2009.

4 Ethical Scientific and Legal issues concerning Stem cell Research", The Irish Council for Bio Ethics, 2008.

5 Ramalho-Santos M and Willenbring H, "On the Origin of the Term "Stem Cell". Cell Stem Cell 1(1): 35–38,(2007).

6 Supra note 4 See Irish.

7 The International Society for Stem Cell Research (ISSCR) is an independent, nonprofit organization formed in 2002 to foster the exchange of information on stem cell research.

8. R Schofield, LG Lajtha, "Determination of the Probability of Self-Renewal in haemopoietic Stem Cells: A Puzzle" Blood Cells , 9: 467-83, (1983).

9 Verfaillie CM., Pera M.F. and Lansdorp P.M. Stem cells: hype and reality. Hematology 1:369-91,(2002).

10 McLaren A. Stem Cells: Golden Opportunities With Ethical Baggage. Science, 288(5472):1778,(2000).

11 Ethical aspects of Human Stem cell Research and Use," Opinion Of The European Group On Ethics In Science and New Technologies To the European Commission,(2004).

12 Id.

13 "Stem Cell Research and Applications Monitoring the Frontiers of Biomedical Research" Produced by the American Association for the Advancement of Science and Institute for Civil Society.1999.

14 Ibid.

15 Evans M.J. and Kaufman M.H. Establishment in Culture of Pluripotential Cells from MouseE mbryos. Nature Jul 9; 292(5819):154-6,(1981).

16 Thomson J.A., Itskovitz-Eldor J., Shapiro S.S,Waknitz M.A, Swiergiel

JJ., Marshall V.S., and Jones JM. Embryonic Stem Cell Lines Derived from Human Blastocysts. Science, Nov 6; 282(5391):1145-7,(1998).

17 Donovan P.J. and Gearhart J. The End of the Beginning for Pluripotent Stem Cells. Nature 414(6859):92-7, 2001.

18 Stem cell Information leaflet , Irish Council on Bio Ethics, 2008 available on http://www.bioethics.ie/uploads/docs/stemcellscience.pdf last visited on 3-06-2009.

19 Derek Morgan, Issues in Medical Law and Ethics, Cavendish, London (2001).

20 Science Meets With The Law, Ian Wilmut, Roslin Research Publication, News, Current Science, Vol. 85, No. 11, 517- Meeting Report),2003.

21 Id.

22 Cloning Fact Sheet available on http://www.ornl.gov/sci/techresources/Human_Genome/elsi/cloning.shtml Last visited on 7-05-2009.

23 "Human Stem Cell Research and the Potential for Clinical Application" National Bioethics Advisory Commission, 2001.

24 Key Ethical Issues in Embryonic Stem Cell Research, Current Issues Brief No. 5 2002–03, information and research services, Australia.

25 Stem Cells, available on http://communicatingscience.aaas.org/Documents/Qs%20and%20AAAs%20about%20Stem%20Cells_3.09.pdf Last visited on 5-05-2009.

26 Stem Cells and the Future of Regenerative Medicine. Committee on the Biological and Biomedical Applications of Stem Cell Research. Board on Life Sciences, National Research Council, Board on Neuroscience and Behavioral Health, Institute of Medicine. Washington DC: National Academics Press; 2002. Available at http://www.nap.edu/catalog/10195.html. Last visited on 4-06-2009.

27 Kiessling A.A. and Anderson, S. Human Embryonic Stem Cells. An Introduction to the Science and Therapeutic Potential. Massachusets: Jones and Bartlett Publishers, Inc., p164,(2003).

28 Uman Embryonic Stem Cell Research, On The Path To An Investment Framework, The Church of England Ethical Advisory Group, April 2003.

29 Ibid.

30 Human Cloning and Dignity : An Ethical Enquiry, The President's Council on Bioethics, 2002.

31 Discussion Paper: Stem cell therapy: the ethical issues, Nuffield Council on Bioethics, November 2001.

32 Key Ethical Issues in Embryonic Stem Cell Research, Current Issues

Brief, No. 5 2002–03, INFORMATION AND RESEARCH SERVICES.

33 S. Sherwin, No Longer Patient: Feminist Ethics and Health Care, Temple University Press, Philadelphia, p. 174–75,(1992).

34 The survey of views presented by Mary Anne Warren in 'IVF and Women's Interests: An Analysis of Feminist Concerns', Bioethics, no. 2, pp. 37–57,(1988).

35 Donna Dickenson, 'Property and Women's Alienation from Their Own Reproductive Labour', Bioethics, vol. 15, no. 3, 2001. Also, Suzzanne Holland, 'Beyond the Embryo: A Feminist Appraisal of the Embryonic Stem cell Debate' in Holland, et al., eds, The Human Embryonic Stem Cell Debate, op. cit.

36 Christine Mummery, Human Embryonic Stem Cells: Research, Ethics and policy, Human Reproduction, Vol. 18, No. 4, 672-682, April 2003.

37 Egg Extraction For Stem Cell Research: Issues for Women's Health, Center for Genetics and Society, May 2006.

38 The medications used to stimulate your ovaries may cause side effects. These side effects can range from mild to severe. Excessive stimulation of the ovaries is called ovarian hyperstimulation.

39 American Society of Reproductive Medicine (ASRM) 2005 Patient's fact sheet: side effects of gonadotropins. Available on http://www.asrm.org/ Patients/FactSheets/Gonadatrophins-Fact.pdf last visited on 5-07-2009.

40 Hugues N Ovarian Stimulation for Assisted Reproductive Technologies. In: Vayena E, Rowe PJ, Griffi n PD (eds) Current Practices and Controversies in Assisted Reproduction. World Health Organization, Geneva, Switzerland, p.102–125, 2002.

41 Supra note 34.

42 Parisian S Open Letter.available on http://www.genetics-and-society.org/ resources/items/200502_letter_parisian.html last visited on 3-06-2009.

43 Steigenga MJ, Helmerhorst FM, DE Koning J et al. 2006 Evolutionary Conserved Structures as Indicators of Medical Risk: Increased Incidence of Cervical Ribs after Ovarian Hyperstimulation in Mice. Animal Biology 56, 63–68,1987.

44 Womens Eggs and Stem Cell Research, Center For Genetics and Society,USA available on http://geneticsandsociety.org/downloads/ Eggs.pdf Last visited on 5-06-2009.

45 The Stem Cell Research Debate: What are Women's Concerns, Association for Womens Rigt in Development ,available on http://www.awid.org/eng/issues-and-analysis/library/the-stem-cell-research-

debate-what-are-women-s-concerns2/(language)/eng-gb Last visited on 7-06-2009.

46 Editorial, Safeguards for Donors. Nature 442(7103): 601,(2006).

47 Holy See Mission. Holy See's call for a Ban on all Human Cloning: UN Speech by Archbishop Migliore; 2003 Sep 30. At : http://www.catholic.org/featured/headline.php?ID=385.

48 Deobra L. Spar, "The Baby Business: How Money, Science, And Politics Drive The Commerce Of Conception" Harvard Business School Press, p 176, 2006.

49 Hwang WS, Ryu YJ, Park JH, "Evidence of a Pluripotent Embryonic Stem cCll line Derived from a Cloned Blastocyst. Science 303, 1669–1674, (2004).

50 Hwang WS, Roh SI, Lee BC, Patient-Specific Embryonic Stem Cells derived from Human SCNT Blastocysts. Science 308, 1777–1783, (2005).

51 Steinbrook R "Egg Donation and Human Embryonic Stem-Cell Research. New England Journal of Medicine 354, 324–326,(2006).

52 Rebecca Dresse, Stem Cell Research Women Who Donate Eggs for Research also Deserve Premium Care, ST. LOUIS POST-DISPATCH Tuesday, Mar 1, 2005, available on <http://www.etopiamedia.net/empnn/pdfs/norsigian5.pdf >last visited on 4-06-2009.

53 Ethical and Policy Issues in Research involving Human Participants, Volume II Commissioned Papers and Staff analysis, 20001 II.

54 Klinger F.G., De Felici M. In vitro Development of Growing Oocytes from Fetal Mouse Oocytes: Stage- Specific Regulation by Stem Cell Factor and Granulose Cells. 244:85-95,(2002).

55 Kirsty Horsey, Human Embryos Cloned using immature eggs, available on http://www.ivf.net/ivf/human_embryos_cloned_using_immature_eggs-o1498.html last visited on 9-06-2009.

56 Hubner K., Fuhrmann G., Christenson L.K., Kehler J., Reinbold R., De La Fuente R. et al. Derivation of Oocytes from Mouse Embryonic Stem Cells. 300:1251-6,(2003). Testa G., Harris J. Ethical Aspects of ES Cell-derived Gametes. 305:1719, (2004).

57 House of Lords Stem Cell Research Report, 2004.

58 Adam, D., Britain Banks on Embryonic Stem Cells to gain Competitive Edge. Nature, 416, 3–4, 2002.

59 Aldhous, P., Regenerative Medicine: A world of Difference. Nature, 414, 838, 2001.

60 Article 40.3.3 of the Irish Constitution expressly prohibits research on

embryos. It acknowledges the right to life of the unborn and states that it is equal to that of the mother.

61 In Austria, however, the import of existing hES cell lines is not prohibited. A majority of the members of the Bioethics Commission are in favour of allowing research on imported ES cell lines created before a set date. Bioethics Commission at the federal Chancellery of 3 April and 8 May 2002. Stem cell research in the context of the EU's Sixth Framework Programme Research. Available at: http://www.austria.gv.at/2004/4/18/stem_cell_research.pdf. last visited on 6-05-2009.

62 The Norwegian Biotechnology Advisory Board. Biotechnology Act 1994. available at http://www.bion.no/lov/lov-19940805-056-eng.pdf. Last visited on 5-06-2009.

63 Group of Advisers on the Ethical Implications of Biotechnology to the European Commission (1997) Ethical aspects of cloning techniques. Opinion No.9. Brussels, p.7.

64 Id.

65 The UNESCO Universal Declaration on the Human Genome And Human Rights states that "Practices which are contrary to human dignity, such as reproductive cloning of human beings, shall not be Permitted"; Article 1 of the Additional Protocol to the Council of Europe Convention on Human Rights and Biomedicine provides that "any intervention seeking to create a human being genetically identical to another human being whether living or dead is prohibited"; and Article 3 (2) of the Charter of Fundamental Rights of the European Union states that the prohibition of the reproductive cloning of human beings must be respected. There is no directly relevant provision in the European Convention on Human Rights. Some have argued that restrictions on reproductive technology could violate the right to respect for private and family life contained in Article 8 (1) but no one has yet sought to test this proposition.

66 Convention for the protection of Human Rights and dignity of the human being with regard to the application of biology and medicine: Convention on Human Rights and Biomedicine.

67 Id Art 18.1.

68 Id Art 18.2.

69 59/280. United Nations Declaration on Human Cloning, 2005.

70 Id Preamble.

71 SB 1260 (Standards for Egg Retrieval for Stem Cell Research) Fact Sheet, 2006.

72 Ibid.

73 Id.

74 The stem cell research debate: What are women's concerns? http://www.awid.org/eng/Issues-and-Analysis/Library/The-stem-cell-research-debate-What-are-women-s-concerns2/(language)/eng-GBLast visited on 5-04-2009.

75 Universal Declaration of Human Rights 1948 Preamble says "Whereas recognition of the inherent dignity and of the equal and inalienable rights of all members of the human family is the foundation of freedom, justice and peace in the world.

76 The Charter of Fundamental Rights of European Union 2000/C 364/01, Art 1 Human dignity is inviolable. It must be respected and protected.

77 Immanuel Kant, General Introduction to the Metaphysic of Morals (1785).

78 Schulman A Bioethics and Human Dignity. The President's Council on Bioethics Staff Working Paper,2005 . Available online at: http://bioethicsprint. bioethics.gov/background/human _ dignity.html, last visited on 4 -04-2009.

79 Report on health Systems research, Bio Medical Research,and Development and regulation of Drugs and Threapeutics available on http://www.adi-media.com/pdf/MB/Healthcare.pdf last visited on 5-07-2009.

80 Guidelines for Stem Cell Research and Therapy, Department of Bio Technology and ICMR, 2007.

81 Id 5.1.

82 Id 5.2.

83 Id 5.3.

84 Id 6.046 Categorization of research on stem cells.

85 Id 6.1.1.

86 Id 4.0 Mechanism for review and monitoring.

87 Id 4.2.

88 Id 4.3.

89 S.S. Agarwal, Regulating Stem Cell Research & Therapy, Indian J Med Res 124, September 2006, pp 225-228.

90 Id.

91 Id 11.1The IC-SCRT/IEC, should review the process of procurement of gametes, lastocysts, or somatic cells for the purpose of generating

new hES cell lines, including procurement of blastocysts in excess of clinical need from infertility clinics. Blastocysts made through IVF specifically for research purposes, and oocytes, sperm, and somatic cells donated for development of hES cell lines derived through SCNT or by parthenogenesis or androgenesis or any other technique should have approval of NAC-SCRT. 11.2 Consent for donation of supernumerary embryos should be obtained from each donor at least 24 hours in advance and not at the time of donation itself. Even people who have given prior indication of their intent to donate blastocysts that remain unutilized after clinical care should give fresh informed consent at the time of donation of the embryo for establishment of hES cell line. Donors should be informed that they retain the right to withdraw consent until the blastocysts are actually used in cell line derivation.

92 Id 8.0.

93 Supra note 80 11.4.

94 Id 11.5.

95 Supra note 93.

96 Pellegrino E.D. Balancing Science, Ethics and Politics: Stem Cell Research, a Paradigm Case. J Contemp Health Law Policy 18(3):591-611,2002.

97 http://geneticsandsociety.org/downloads/Eggs.pdf Last visited on 5-06-2009.

98 Id.

99 ASRM is a multidisciplinary organization dedicated to the advancement of the art, science, and practice of reproductive medicine. The Society accomplishes its mission through the pursuit of excellence in education and research and through advocacy on behalf of patients, physicians, and affiliated health care providers. The Society is committed to facilitating and sponsoring educational activities for the lay public and continuing medical education activities for professionals who are engaged in the practice of and research in reproductive medicine.

100 Rebecca Dresse, Stem Cell Research: Women who donate eggs for research also deserve premium care, ST. LOUIS POST-DISPATCH Tuesday, Mar 1, 2005, available on http://www.etopiamedia.net/empnn/pdfs/norsigian5.pdf last visited on 3-07-2009.

4

Abortion : Balancing Women's Fundamental Reproductive Rights And Right of Unborn

In a case that led to a nationwide debate on abortion laws, Niketa and her husband Haresh, with the help of their gynaecologist had filed a petition seeking permission to abort her foetus after learning it had a heart disorder during an echocardiogram in the 24th week of pregnancy.[1] Their lawyer pleaded that surgery to implant a pacemaker and then further surgeries to change it every five years would be economically unviable for the Mehtas, besides being traumatic for the child. The MTP Act, 1971, does not permit termination of pregnancy after 20 weeks. The court rejected her plea. Days later, Niketa had a miscarriage While Niketa failed to obtain a favourable judgement from the court, her case has prompted the government to announce that it will be considering a review of the law.

In another landmark verdict the Supreme Court allowed a mentally challenged orphan girl who was raped at a Nari Niketan in Chandigarh to continue her pregnancy resulting from the sexual assault. The apex court was initially reluctant to interfere with a Punjab and Haryana High Court order directing medical termination of the pregnancy. But it changed its mind after counsel crafted the arguments based both on law and emotional grounds.[2] Earlier this 19 year old mentally challenged woman kept at Nari Niketan, Chandigarh which is a government institution for destitute women, was raped sometime in March 2009 on the premises by the security guards and conceived. In May 2009 the pregnancy was detected. The rape was widely reported in the media. Despite that no institution or individual came forward to assist or support the woman. In the same month the Director of the Government Medical College and Hospital constituted a three member Board consisting of a psychiatrist, a clinical psychologist and a special educator to evaluate the mental status of the woman. Their report did not suggest anything out of the ordinary except for the observation that "she also cries almost daily". The Board found that her mental age came out to be 9 years and that she fell in the category of mild mental retardation. A few days later, a four doctor Multi Disciplinary Medical Board was constituted which included a psychiatrist and the Board submitted a report recommending medical termination of pregnancy. But what was unfortunate is that all these process culminated in a great deal of delay causing lot of trauma for the victim.

Such instances are widespread in other parts of the world too in a striking incident a six months pregnant and feeling unwell, a poor woman goes to a state-run clinic in Rio de Janeiro for help—and is turned away, a week later, she is dead. These cases raises several ethical dilemmas related to reproductive rights and specially abortion, All of these women were denied their reproductive rights and suffered because of it. But does that mean their human rights were violated as well this is the focus of this paper.

Significance of Re-productive Rights

In every historical period and everywhere, reproduction has provided an important topic of ethical reflection specially from the point of view of women. There are two basic ethical perspectives in this context. The individual point of view, based in the human rights tradition based on autonomy and dignity. The emphasis tends to be on personal rights and welfare, and the extent to which actions and policies promote them. Secondly the collective point of view, concerned mostly with population issues and the aggregate results of individual behaviours on health and demography. The emphasis tends to be on utilitarian approach promoting the maximum happiness. [3]

With the positive definition of health as a state of complete physical, mental, and social well being and not merely the absence of disease or infirmity, reproductive health became a significant focus area of Human right agenda. Though various opinions exist reproductive rights are said to consist

1. The freedom to decide whether, when and how many children to have;
2. The right to modern family planning information and modern family planning methods;
3. The right to control one's own sexuality.

In the discourse on reproduction women's role gained attention because of the central role she has in reproduction and secondly the major burden of reproductive and other medical ill health generally falls on women. In fact historically women always occupied the lower position in reproductive health ladder shaped by social relationships, on custom, and tradition.

It is further to be noted that reproductive ill health is different from other forms of ill health because of the centrality of intimate human behaviors. Human sexual and reproductive behaviors are heavily dependent on social relationships, on custom, tradition, and taboo. It is therefore inevitable that social groups and individuals with the least power, with the most limited ability to make decisions, [4] with the most constrained capacities for choice, will suffer the major portion of the burden of ill health resulting from these behaviors and relationships. To give just one example, we know that the major burden of death and disability relating to sexuality and reproduction falls on women. Among women of reproductive age in developing countries, over 36% of healthy years of life lost are due to three conditions associated with sex and reproduction: maternal mortality and morbidity, sexually transmitted diseases, and HIV/ AIDS. Among men, the figure is only 12%.[5] Biologically, women are vulnerable because they undergo the risks of childbearing, and they are more at risk of contracting sexually transmitted diseases. They are also less likely to receive treatment in a timely manner because of the low social status.

Recognizing the reproductive rights has various advantages For Individuals this is highly related to his autonomy and offers the benefit of for families, the ability to choose family size offers increased choice as to the use of family resources, education, and employment. For communities, individual choices can result in increased options for economic and social development.[6] It should also be noted that even in jurisdictions which has granted reproductive rights and liberty including abortion there is an extreme dissonance between the wide availability of reproductive services and its inaccessibility to women on the social and economic margins. Though legal, it remains out of reach for thousands of women each year who find that the expense, location, and shortage of services, burdensome legal restrictions, and further anti reproductive threats and violence create daunting barriers. It is imperative that reproductive rights percolate to the lower strata including women.

Abortion: Issues and Arguments

Medically, it is defined as a miscarriage or induced termination of pregnancy.[7] Induced abortion has been going for centuries According to United Nations from 1920-2008 a total of 858,000,000 reported abortions, and an estimated 961,000,000 total abortions took place **(Table 1)**.

Most of this unreported abortions are illegal. It is widely acknowledged that in countries in which abortion is legally restricted, women seek abortions clandestinely, under conditions that are medically unsafe and therefore life threatening. According to the World Health Organization (WHO), about 20 million women have unsafe abortions every year.[8] These unsafe abortions are responsible for the deaths of nearly 70,000 women annually.[9]

Throughout history, induced abortions have been a source of considerable debate and controversy. On the one hand supporters believed that it is a woman's individual rights, right to her life, to her liberty, and to the pursuit of her happiness, that sanctions her right to have an abortion. Their argument is related to Bodily Sovereignty. Each woman has the sole right to make decisions about what happens to her body - no one should force her either to carry or terminate a pregnancy against her will. Second arguments are in relation to the health. There are situations where abortions is done to safeguard the life of a fetus, as it would involve risk if pregnancy is carried, it might damage the fetus resulting in danger to the life of the mother. The continuance of the pregnancy would involve risk to the life of the pregnant woman greater than if the pregnancy were terminated. The termination is necessary to prevent grave permanent injury to the physical or mental health of the pregnant woman. Nearly all abortions take place in the first trimester, when a fetus cannot exist independent of the mother and is not in the stage of fetal personhood.[10]

Fetal personhood refers to certain concept of the law that

Table 1. Summary of Registered Abortions Worldwide, through October 2008

Country	year range of reported data	total reported abortions	estimated total for missing data, under-reporting	estimated additional abortions to Oct. 2008	most recent annual abortion figure	estimated total abortions through October 2008
Albania	1975-2006	578,622	54,668	17,508	9,552	650,798
Andorra	1995	99		1,270	99	1,369
Anguilla	2002-2005	98		59	21	157
Armenia	1992-2006	281,827	156,168	20,404	11,132	458,399
Australia	1970-2007	1,728,500		59,860	71,861	1,788,360
Austria	1960-2001	594,251		16,358	2,394	610,609
Azerbaijan	1992-2006	357,487		38,249	20,867	395,736
Bahrain	1997-2007	10,229		8,770	1,766	18,999
Barbados	1992-1995	1,000	1,000	5,133	400	7,133
Belarus	1992-2006	2,060,320		107,259	58,516	2,167,579
Belgium	1968-2006	372,651	49,876	31,893	17,867	454,420
Belize	1985-1996	8,609	7,186	30,801	2,603	46,596
Bermuda	1982-1983	177		2,284	92	2,461
Bosnia and Herzegovina	2001	1,201	10,809	8,206	1,201	20,216
Botswana	1980-1984	66	18	405	17	489

Bulgaria	1953-2006	5,594,536		68,319	37,272	5,662,855
Canada	1968-2005	2,893,870		274,271	96,815	3,168,141
Channel Islands	1968-2007	12,455		30	37	12,485
Chile	1986-1991	281		1,127	67	1,408
ROC Taiwan	1967-1999	45,884	667,395	373,476	42,282	1,086,755
PR China	1971-2006	299,571,678	10,000,000	13,396,691	7,308,615	322,968,369
Cocos Islands	1978	2		59	2	61
Costa Rica	1995-2005	95,255		22,590	7,974	117,845
Croatia	1992-2006	258,817		18,696	10,200	277,513
Cuba	1968-2005	4,431,170	105,483	177,147	62,530	4,713,800
Czech Republic	1993-2006	3,374,079		73,320	40,000	3,447,399
Czechoslovakia	1953-1992	3,676,501				3,676,501
Denmark	1939-2006	822,089		27,600	15,061	849,689
Dominican Republic	1995-2005	221,990	51,255	82,630	29,167	355,875
Estonia	1992-2006	258,180		17,219	9,394	275,399
Faeroe Islands	1966-2006	860	747	75	41	1,682
Finland	1951-2006	611,340		19,512	10,645	630,852
France	1936-2006	5,959,461	1,148	384,422	209,740	6,345,031
French Guiana	1984-2006	23,884	1,916	3,508	1,914	29,308
Georgia	1992-2006	399,065		38,866	21,204	437,931
FR Germany	1944-2007	3,740,353	51,311	96,890	116,315	3,888,554

East Germany	1948-1989	1,744,445				1,744,445
Gibraltar	1981-2005	194	304	22	8	520
Greece	1971-2003	193,383	12,575	76,322	15,792	282,280
Greenland	1967-2005	24,249	200	2,546	899	26,995
Guadeloupe	1976-2006	83,378	4,100	8,479	4,626	95,957
Guyana	1970-2003	43,614	124,476	21,748	4,500	189,838
Hong Kong	1973-2005	492,972	19,557	40,200	14,190	552,729
Hungary	1949-2006	5,925,784		116,762	63,700	6,042,546
Iceland	1960-2005	24,137		2,456	867	26,593
India	1972-2000	13,841,201		5,664,371	723,142	19,505,572
Isle of Man	1968-2007	5,176		112	135	5,288
Israel	1979-2006	500,008		36,348	19,830	536,356
Italy	1968-2004	4,403,860		525	137	4,404,385
Japan	1949-2005	36,802,431	30,000,000	819,096	289,127	67,621,527
Kazakhstan	1992-2006	2,669,774		239,387	130,599	2,909,161
ROK South Korea	1961-1999	4,566,700	9,721,050	1,875,245	212,300	16,162,995
Kosovo	2005-2006	11,154		3,026	1,651	14,180
Kyrgyzstan	1992-2006	462,139		27,337	14,914	489,476
Latvia	1992-2006	313,469		21,675	11,825	335,144
Lithuania	1992-2006	326,532		17,479	9,536	344,011
Macedonia	1994-2006	133,838		11,298	6,164	145,136
Martinique	1976-2006	58,026	5,554	4,384	2,392	67,964
Mexico	1980-2006	64,826	18,000	1,464	799	84,290

Moldova	1992-2006	522,683		28,873	15,752	551,556
Mongolia	1984-2006	337,737		23,084	12,594	360,821
Montenegro	2006	1,699		3,114	1,699	4,813
Netherlands	1968-2006	786,718		52,187	28,471	838,905
New Caledonia	1997-1998	2,994		14,415	1,466	17,409
New Zealand	1964-2006	356,188		32,873	17,934	389,061
Norway	1954-2006	554,517		25,918	14,140	580,435
Panama	1972-2000	159	218	86	11	463
Panama Canal Zone	1970-1978	398				398
Poland	1955-2006	6,384,057		633	350	6,384,690
Portugal	1972-2005	10,178		2,600	925	12,778
Puerto Rico	1991-2005	77,717	150,891	19,026	6,716	247,634
Qatar	1995-2005	1,380		504	183	1,884
Reunion	1976-2006	132,154		8,290	4,523	140,444
Romania	1958-2006	21,065,391	826,149	275,400	150,246	22,166,940
Russia	1992-2004	32,045,451		6,890,093	1,797,572	38,935,544
Saint Helena	1985-1990	61		89	5	150
Serbia	1992-2006	914,570	53,844	47,043	25,665	1,015,457
Seychelles	1997-2006	4,465		812	443	5,277
Singapore	1970-2006	548,501		22,054	12,032	570,555
Slovakia	1993-2006	381,739		34,925	19,054	416,664
Slovenia	1992-2006	133,781		10,323	5,632	144,104
South Africa	1971-2005	552,005	886	245,397	86,621	798,288

Spain	1941-2005	1,284,724	377,716	252,237	89,049	1,914,677
Suriname	1994	262		3,624	262	3,886
Sweden	1939-2007	1,350,433		30,492	36,606	1,380,925
Switzerland	1966-2005	397,521		30,531	10,781	428,052
Tajikistan	1992-2006	396,630		32,077	17,500	428,707
Trust Territory of the Pacific Islands	1970	2		44		46
Tunisia	1965-2003	537,414	72,050	77,328	16,000	686,792
Turkey	1993-2003	768,709	2,078,600	709,484	146,800	3,556,793
Turkmenistan	1992-2006	372,396		27,053	14,759	399,449
Turks and Caicos Islands	2005	188	202	90	32	480
U.S.S.R.	1922-1991	287,872,383	10,084,237			297,956,620
Ukraine	1992-2006	7,884,890		420,889	229,618	8,305,779
United Kingdom	1958-2007	6,104,441		159,912	208,422	6,264,353
United States	1926-2007	47,671,878		2,540,876	1,206,200	50,212,754
Uzbekistan	1992-2006	1,304,700		82,485	45,000	1,387,185
Venezuela	1968	3,085		122,884	3,085	125,969
Vietnam	1976-2006	20,904,023	922,900	802,500	500,000	22,629,423
Yugoslavia	1955-1991	5,396,261				5,396,261
Zambia	1983	1,200		29,799	1,200	30,999
Subtotals	1922-2007	857,743,860	65,632,489	37,475,233	14,472,144	960,851,582

Source : Global Abortion Summary

considers the fetus a separate unborn person, rather than a part of the woman carrying the fetus. [11] Historically, the fetus only acquired legal rights separate from those of the woman at birth.[12] Later multiple jurisdictions considered measures concerning criminal punishments for harm to a fetus or embryo independent of the harm to the pregnant woman.[13] These provisions are pointed out to oppose abortion right of women. But it is to be remembered that the concept of personhood is different from the concept of human life. Human life occurs at conception, but fertilized eggs used for in vitro fertilization are also human lives and those not implanted are routinely thrown away. Is this murder, and if not, then how is abortion murder.

Arguments against abortion range from objections based on various constitution's protection of the right to human life all the way to the biblical bases for the belief that human life begins at conception. This elevates the sanctity of human life to a protective status and overrides the right of anyone to terminate another human life for their own convenience abortion can result in medical complications later in life; the risk of ectopic pregnancies doubles, and the chance of a miscarriage and Pelvic Inflammatory Disease also increases.[14]

There is a further dimension to abortion laws which many of the opposing group points out. They point out that if unlimited liberties of abortion are guaranteed. It may encourage sex-selective abortion which poses serious threats to society as a whole. Sex-selection may be harming women as a class, if female fetuses are selectively aborted. Whereas various reproductive rights give women control over whether and when to have children, sex-selection gives men greater control over women's reproduction and the sexual composition of future generations, and increases the risks of harm discrimination, and subordination to all women. Thus, instead of eliminating subordination, sex-selection increases social, economic, political and reproductive exploitation.[15] This is evident in countries like India where full scale abortions rights are not even granted. In

India states like Haryana is facing serious threats and change in demographic structure the situation is so grim that women has to be brought from outside. These many point out that legally permissible and morally justified. The dangers of sex-selection are that it will create a demographic imbalance and lead to a targeting of women's reproduction as a means of gender demographic politics. Sex-selection also creates distributive concerns, as only wealthier women will have access to the technology, so that females that are born will be "poorer and darker," exacerbating class inequalities.[16]

International Legislative Approach

Reproductive rights including right to abortion are internationally recognized as critical both to advancing women's human rights and to promoting development. In recent years, governments from all over the world have acknowledged and pledged to advance reproductive rights to an unprecedented degree. Reproductive rights were clarified and finally endorsed internationally in the Cairo Consensus that emerged from the 1994 International Conference on Population and Development.

Even before this development various human right doctrines can be interpreted as including reproductive and associated rights. Article 25 (1) of Universal Declaration of Human Rights (UDHR)[17] affirms that everyone has a right to a standard of living adequate for the health of himself and his family, including food, clothing, housing and medical care and necessary social services, and the right to security in the event of unemployment, sickness, disability, widowhood, old age or other lack of livelihood in circumstances beyond his control.[18] This provision can be positively interpreted to include right to reproductive services. International Covenant on Economic Social and Cultural Rights (ICESCR)[19] which followed UDHR also to an extent recognized this right. Article 12 of the ICESCR recognizes the right of everyone to the highest standard of physical and sexual health. Governments are required to take all steps necessary to reduce stillbirths and maternal deaths.[20]

The Convention on the Rights of the Child (CRC) recognizes the responsibility of governments to promote the rights of children.[21] At the same time it also promotes the right to family planning services. Article 24 requires government to ensure appropriate prenatal and postnatal health care for mothers.[22] Article 34 requires governments to protect the child from all forms of sexual exploitation and sexual abuse, and asks governments to take all effective and appropriate measures with a view to abolishing traditional practices that harm the health of children. Nearly all governments have signed this convention. It is therefore a strong tool for holding governments accountable with regard to the right recognized.[23]

The Convention on the Elimination of All Forms of Discrimination against Women (CEDAW) for the first time articulated comprehensively womens rights.[24] Article 12 of CEDAW requires the states to eliminate discrimination against women in access to health services throughout their life cycle, particularly in the areas of family planning, pregnancy and childbirth. The Convention stressed that access to health care, including reproductive health, is a basic right. It also called on governments to provide appropriate services relating to pregnancy, birth and breast-feeding.[25] Article 12 (1) states that governments shall take all appropriate measures to eliminate discrimination against women in the field of health care to ensure, access to health-care services, including those related to family planning. Article 12 (2) ensure to women appropriate services in connection with pregnancy, confinement and the post-natal period, granting free services where necessary, as well as adequate nutrition during pregnancy and lactation. States Parties [26]are encouraged to address the issue of women's health throughout the woman's lifespan. The articles of the convention are applicable to women, including girls and adolescents. In 1999, the Committee on the Elimination of All Forms of

Discrimination against Women[27] interpreted Article 12 of the Convention, which requires states to eliminate discrimination against women in access to health services throughout the life cycle, particularly in the areas of family planning, pregnancy and confinement and during the post-natal period. The Committee affirmed that access to health care, including reproductive health, is a basic right under the Convention, stating, inter alia: "States parties should implement a comprehensive national strategy to promote women's health throughout their lifespan. This will include interventions aimed at both the prevention and treatment of diseases and conditions affecting women, as well as responding to violence against women, and will ensure universal access for all women to a full range of high-quality and affordable health care, including sexual and reproductive health services. The Convention on All Forms of Racial Discrimination also promotes the right to the highest standard of health, including reproductive health in paragraph 5e (IV).[28]

The International Conference on Population and Development 1994 defined and enumerated the contents of reproductive rights.[29] At the ICPD 179 countries agreed on a plan to transform and fund reproductive health programmes. The final document and ICPD's Programme of Action (PoA) call for universal access to basic reproductive health services and specific measures for fostering human development.[30] Reproductive health is defined by the Programme of Action of the International Conference on Population and Development (ICPD) 1994 as "a state of complete physical, mental and social well-being in all matters relating to the reproductive health system and to its function and processes. It implies that people have the capability to reproduce and the freedom to decide if, when and how often to do so."[31] Reproductive health is not merely about the absence of disease or infirmity. Reproductive and sexual rights, according to the ICPD, include human rights already recognized in national laws and in international human rights documents such as the Universal Declaration on Human Rights. They include a person's right to:

- Information, education, skills, support and services needed to make responsible decisions about sexuality consistent with their own values;
- Bodily integrity and voluntary sexual relationships;
- A full range of voluntary and accessible sexual and reproductive health services;
- Decide freely and responsibly the number, spacing and timing of their children and the information and means to do so;
- Attain the highest standard of sexual and reproductive health; and
- Make decisions concerning reproduction free of discrimination, coercion or violence.[32]

Paragraphs 7.6 to 8.3 of ICPD calls on governments to take a number of actions to promote the right of an individual to the highest standard of health, including reproductive health and rights. It declares that everyone has the right to life, liberty and security of person. Reproductive rights also includes couples and individuals right to make decisions concerning reproduction free of discrimination, coercion and violence, as expressed in human rights documents.[33] Government at all levels are urged to institute systems of monitoring and evaluation of user centered services with a view to detecting, preventing and controlling abuses by family-planning managers and providers ... To this end, Governments should secure conformity to human rights and to ethical and professional standards in the delivery of family planning and related reproductive health services aimed at ensuring responsible, voluntary and informed consent and also regarding service provision.[34]

Since the appointment of a Special Rapporteur on violence against women in 1994, the UN has received regular reports on the prevalence of different forms of violence, the legal responses that exist and recommendations for action. The Special Rapporteur on Violence Against Women has also addressed policies and practices that have an impact on women's reproductive rights.[35] The Beijing Platform for Action (BPFA, 1995) and Beijing +5 (2000) The BPFA incorporated much of the ICPD language on reproductive rights. The platform states that "good health is essential to leading a productive and fulfilling life, and the right of all women to control all aspects of their health, in particular their own fertility, is basic to their empowerment."[36] It further states that "the human rights of women include their right to have control over and decide freely and responsibly on matters related to their sexuality, including sexual and reproductive health, free of coercion, discrimination and violence."[37] Following ICPD wide definition has been given to reproductive health it states reproductive health implies that people are able to have a satisfying and safe sex life and that they have the capability to reproduce and the freedom to decide if, when and how often to do so. Implicit in this last condition are the right of men and women to be informed and to have access to safe, effective, affordable and acceptable methods of family planning of their choice, as well as other methods of their choice for regulation of fertility which are not against the law, and the right of access to appropriate health-care services that will enable women to go safely through pregnancy and childbirth and provide couples with the best chance of having a healthy infant.[38] UN Security Council Resolution 1325 has also addressed the While this resolution does not specifically mandate the protection of women's reproductive and sexual health and rights, it does call on all parties to armed conflict to take specific measures to protect women and girls from gender-based violence and the social, economic and health status of women.[39]

This constellation of reproductive rights, embracing fundamental human rights established by earlier treaties, was reaffirmed at various conferences and various international and regional agreements since, as well as in many national laws. They include the right to decide the number, timing and spacing of children, the right to voluntarily marry and establish a family, and the right to the highest attainable standard of living, among others. Generally safe abortion is accepted as part of the reproductive rights of women.

If we look at the specific human right approach to abortion Article 1 of the American Declaration of Rights and Duties of Man and the Inter American Commission of Human Rights say that abortion is legalized until the end of First trimester.[40] Right to life is protected from the moment of its conception by Articles 6(1) of the ICCPR,[41] Article 2 of the European Convention of Human Rights[42] and Article 4 of the African Charter of Human and People's right.[43] But they are silent on the issue of when does life begin. But the interpretations have forced us to believe that the child is not to be protected from the time of its inception. The right to life of the fetus has to be balanced with the rights of the mother. International courts and tribunals have not addressed the difficult philosophical issue of when life begins, but have focused on the meaning of the language used in the relevant treaties. They have generally held that the references to every human being or everyone or every person do not include an unborn foetus.

The WHO defines "health" as "a state of complete physical, mental and social well-being, not merely the absence of disease or infirmity."[44] While the right to health does not guarantee perfect health for all women, it has been interpreted to require governments to provide health care and to work toward creating conditions conducive to the enjoyment of good health.[45] In the context of abortion, this right to health can be interpreted to require governments to take appropriate measures to ensure that women are not exposed to the risks of unsafe abortion. Such measures include removing legal restrictions on abortion and ensuring access to high-quality abortion services.

The Programme of Action adopted at the United Nations International Conference on Population and Development (ICPD) in 1994 called upon governments to consider the consequences of unsafe abortion on women's health. It states that governments should "deal with the health impact of unsafe abortion as a major public health concern."[46] In addition, in a paragraph addressing research on women's health, the Platform for Action urges governments "to understand and better address the determinants and consequences of unsafe abortion."[47] At the 1995 Fourth World Conference on Women, the international community reiterated this language and urged governments to "consider reviewing laws containing punitive measures against women who have undergone illegal abortions."[48] In 1999, at the five-year review of the ICPD, governments approved a provision recognizing the need for greater safety and availability of abortion services. Paragraph 63(iii) calls upon states "take appropriate steps to help women avoid abortion" and to "provide for the humane treatment and counselling of women who have had recourse to abortion".[49] Further General assembly resolution highlighted maternal mortality. Resolution declared that most instances of maternal mortality and morbidity are preventable, and that preventable maternal mortality and morbidity is a health, development and human rights challenge that also requires the effective promotion and protection of the human rights of women and girls, in particular their rights to life, to be equal in dignity, to education, to be free to seek, receive and impart information, to enjoy the benefits of scientific progress, to freedom from discrimination, and to enjoy the highest attainable standard of physical and mental health, including sexual and reproductive health.[50]

Roe v. *Wade* became one of the most politically significant Supreme Court decisions in history, reshaping national politics, dividing the nation into "pro-choice" and "pro-life" camps, and inspiring grassroots activism.[51] This is a landmark United States Supreme Court decision establishing that most laws against abortion violate a constitutional right to privacy, thus overturning all state laws outlawing or restricting abortion that were inconsistent with the decision. Jone Roe, the plaintiff wanted to terminate her pregnancy because she contended that it was a result of rape. Relying on the current state of medical knowledge, the decision established a system of trimesters that attempted to balance the state's legitimate interests with the individual's constitutional rights. The Court ruled that the state cannot restrict a woman's right to an abortion during the first trimester, the state can regulate the abortion procedure during the second trimester "in ways that are reasonably related to maternal health," and in the third trimester, demarcating the viability of the fetus, a state can choose to restrict or even to proscribe abortion as it sees fit.[52]

Also the Abortion Act,1967 of the UK in its Article 2 does not confer an absolute right to life to the unborn.[53] It was held in *Patons* v. *United Kingdom*[54]. Abortion is permitted if the continuance of the pregnancy involves risk. The right to life of fetus is subject to an implied limitation allowing pregnancy to be terminated in order to protect the life of a mother. The same was upheld in *H* v. *Norway*.[55] It was also held in 1992 by the Supreme Court that a women has the same exclusive right to abortion as to any to any other medical treatment. The prospective fathers have no right to be consulted for the same.

While the phrase "right to life" has been associated with the campaigns of those who oppose abortion, it has not been interpreted in any international setting to require restrictions on abortion. Most recently, the European Court of Human Rights, in the case of *Vo v. France*, stated that "it is neither desirable, nor even possible as matters stand, to answer in the abstract the question whether the unborn child is a person for the purpose of Article 2 of the Convention ..." providing that "everyone's right to life shall be protected by law" The court therefore refused to adopt a ruling that would have called into question the validity of laws permitting abortion in 39 member states of the Council of Europe.[56]

In 2006, Colombia's Constitutional Court handed down an unprecedented case overturning the country's criminal abortion ban.[57] The petition before the Court argued that Colombia's Constitution required exceptions to the abortion prohibition to protect women's fundamental rights to life, health privacy, and dignity. It further argued that Colombia's refusal to permit abortion to save a woman's life, or protect her health, or in cases of rape or foetal impairment, was out of step with widely accepted norms that recognize minimum safeguards to protect women's basic human rights.[58]

According to United Nations data for 2001, three countries ban abortion under all circumstances: El Salvador, Malta, and the Vatican City. Of 193 countries examined, 3 ban abortion in all circumstances and 59 officially permit abortion only to save the life of the mother. Officially, 122 countries allow abortion to protect the physical health of the mother, 120 to protect the mother's mental health, 83 in cases of rape or incest, and 76 to eliminate an unhealthy child. Eleven countries allow abortion for economic or social reasons (besides those allowing abortion on demand): Barbados, Belize, Fiji, Finland, Iceland, India, Japan, Luxembourg, Saint Vincent and the Grenadines, the United Kingdom, and Zambia. [59]

While it is our responsibility to advocate the fostering of reproductive health for enabling environments and reproductive rights, it is the responsibility of states to ensure that these rights are realized. Perhaps the best way of describing this responsibility is to describe the worldwide consequences of having failed to successfully promote reproductive health and rights in numerical terms.[60]

- Around 500,000 women die each year from childbirth, and many millions are disabled, yet the overwhelming majority of these deaths and injuries could have been prevented by relatively low-cost improvements in health care.[61]

- Some 20 million women each year risk their lives and health by resorting to unsafe abortion, and almost 80,000 die as a consequence. The majority of these unsafe abortions could have been avoided through improved family planning[62] information and services and increased access to safe termination of pregnancy.
- There are 120-150 million women who want to limit or space their pregnancies but do not have access to contraception. Almost 6 million people are newly infected with HIV.[63] These grim statistics tell a sad story of the consequenc es of the denial of sexual and reproductive rights, especially the right to free choice with regard to sexual.[64]

While reproductive rights are understood to represent a bundle of rights drawn from traditional human rights instruments, reproductive rights as such have not yet been codified as legally binding and enforceable rights. While the human rights treaty bodies have to varying degrees accepted responsibility for monitoring the implementation of reproductive rights, no legal procedures have yet been established to ensure the compliance of states. We must move forward by making reproductive rights as such legally binding for states if reproductive health for all is actually to be achieved.

We must move step by step toward this objective. As a first step, all the provisions relevant to reproductive rights that exist in the present legal human rights instruments could be compiled into a declaration of commitment to reproductive rights endorsed by the international community. This could then prepare the foundation for a convention on reproductive liberty.[65]

Indian Legislative and judicial approach

A woman in Chidika village of Andhra Pradesh, developed pregnancy related complications. Since there was no transportation facility from that village, people had to carry her on a cot to the health centre in the nearby town. It took two hours to reach the health centre. By the time she reached the health centre, there was no staff available to attend her immediately. The woman was in critical condition and died. The above case study illustrates the situation of health services in our country which lag behind in providing basic facilities and accessibility to women during pregnancy. India accounts for the second highest maternal mortality rate in the world.[66]

Table 2. Causes of maternal mortality: India studies and global pattern (% of total deaths by causes)

Source and location	*Registrar General of India 1998*	*Bhatia data 84-85 (Causes of mm in south India)*	*Kumar data 1986 (MM enquiry in rural community of north India)*	*Maine (Safe motherhood program)*
Causes of death	*National*	*Ananthpur district*	*Rural north India*	*Global pattern*
Hemorrhage	29.6	6.8	18.2	28
Anemia	19.0	9.2	16.4	-
Hypertensive disease of pregnancy	8.3	8.0	5.5	17
Puerperal sepsis	16.1	30.5	16.4	11
Abortion	8.9	10.3	9.1	19
Obstructed labour	9.5	4.9	7.3	11
Not classifiable	2.1	-	10.9	15
Other/indirect	6.4	25	10.9	15
MMR per 100000 live birth	407	830	230	

Source: *Prof Dileep Mavalankar* State of Maternal Health in India

Women's general health and reproductive health rights

were brought to the forefront through several positive campaigns led by various womens organizations against the introduction of hazardous contraceptives like EP drugs, Net En, Norplant, Depo-Provera, sex selective abortions and coercive population control policies of the State. Women's groups raised questions on the safety of hormonal contraceptive technologies, of the way in which clinical trials were carried out, on notions of informed consent and on general issues of women's health in the context of India's Family Welfare Programme. Furthermore, women's health activists interminably criticised the fact that women were only addressed by the health care system as reproductive beings, and their other health needs were largely ignored.[67]

In response to this The Mother and Child Health (MCH), nutrition and immunization programmes were brought under the umbrella of the Family Welfare Programme and was finally transformed into the Reproductive Child Health (RCH) programme.[68] The national RCH programme was launched in 1997 to provide integrated health and family welfare services for women and children. The programme aimed at improving the quality, distribution and accessibility of services and to meet the health care needs of women in the reproductive ages and children more effectively. The components included:

- prevention and management of unwanted pregnancy;
- services to promote safe motherhood and child survival;
- nutritional services for vulnerable groups;
- prevention and treatment of reproductive tract infections (RTIs) andsexually transmitted infections (STIs);
- reproductive health services for adolescents;
- health, sexuality and gender information, education and counselling;
- establishment of effective referral systems;[69]

Despite these programmes and the existing reproductive health care services, there were certain issues that have been completely neglected and ignored by the experts. Women are unable to seek care for problems, which are not related to pregnancy and other gynecological complications that are part of reproductive rights like spacing of children, the decision when to have a baby. In addition to this, the programmes deny a commitment to respond to women's health needs throughout the life cycle and to go beyond the constricted conceptualisation of their reproductive roles as concerned only with child bearing.[70]

If we analyze the legislative framework the Constitution of India does not explicitly recognize health as a Fundamental Right .The only article which can be interpreted to include right to health is Article 21 of the Constitution of India .It guarantees the Right to Life of every citizen, and imposes the duty to protect this right upon the state.[71] The Supreme Court of India has many times stated that the right to life includes the right to live with dignity and all that goes along with it, [72] Thus these constitutional provisions can be interpreted expansively to understand and ensure women's right to reproductive health. Further some guidance can be obtained from directive principles of State Policy. Article 47 states that it is the Duty of the State to raise the level of nutrition and the standard of living and to improve public health.[73]

The direct Indian legislative approach regarding abortion is contained under Section 312 of the Indian Penal Code, and the medical termination of pregnancy Act(MTP) 1971. IPC defines the offence of 'causing miscarriage' as follows "whoever voluntarily causes a woman with child to miscarry shall, if such miscarriage be not caused in good faith for the purpose of saving the life of the woman, be punished with imprisonment of either description for a term which may extend to 3 years, or with fine, or with both; and, if the woman be quick with child, shall be punished with imprisonment of either description for a term which may extend to 7 years, and shall also be liable to fine. [74]

The MTP Act came into being after Shantilal Shah Committee recommended liberalization of abortion law in 1966 to reduce maternal morbidity and mortality associated with illegal abortion. On these bases, in 1969 Medical termination of pregnancy bill was introduced in Rajya Sabha and Lok Sabha and passed by Indian Parliament in Aug. 1971. Medical Termination Of Pregnancy Act, 1971 (MTP Act) was implemented from Apr.1972.[75] Implemented rules and regulations were again revised in 1975 to eliminate time consuming procedures for the approval of the place and to make services more readily available. The Act is encapsulated in 8 sections, concisely setting forth the law on this subject. While the first two sections set out the scope and clarify certain terms in the Act, the operative section would be the third, which lays down the conditions when pregnancy may be terminated by a medical practitioner. Section 4 defines the place where pregnancy may be terminated while the fifth section sets out cases where sections 3 and 4 would not apply. Section 6 and 7 empower the Central Government to make rules and regulations respectively while section 8 protects any action taken or any damage caused under this Act by any registered medical *practitioner* acting in good faith.[76]

The preamble of the Act states "that it is an Act to provide for the termination of certain pregnancies by registered medical practitioners and for matters connected therewith or incidental thereto". This law guarantees the Right of Women in India to terminate an unintended pregnancy by a registered medical practitioner in a hospital established or maintained by the Government or a place being approved for the purpose of this Act by the Government. Not all pregnancies could be terminated.

Section 3 of the said Act, says that pregnancy can be terminated :

(a) Where the length of the pregnancy does not exceed 12 weeks if such medical practitioner is, or

(b) Where the length of the pregnancy exceeds 12 weeks but does not exceed 20 weeks, if not less than 2 registered medical practitioners are of opinion, formed in good faith that

1: The continuance of the pregnancy would involve a risk to the life of the pregnant women or

2: A risk of grave injury to the her physical or mental health ;or

3: If the pregnancy is caused by rape; or

4: There exist a substantial risk that, if the child were born it would suffer from some physical or mental abnormalities so as to be seriously handicapped; or

5: Failure of any device or method used by the married couple for the purpose of limiting the number of children; or

6: Risk to the health of the pregnant woman by the reason of her actual or reasonably foreseeable environment.[77]

The second sub section is the operative section of the Act and the one that lays down the time during which the termination could be performed. It allows termination of regnancy within 12 weeks of conception. If it exceeds such period, but is within 20 weeks, then a special case should be shown to be present, as provided by the section. Thus, abortion beyond the prescribed statutory limit of 20 weeks would be illegal.[78]

In short termination of pregnancy is allowed (1) As a health measure when there is danger to the life or risk to physical or mental health of the women;

(2) On humanitarian grounds - such as when pregnancy arises from a sex crime like rape or intercourse with a lunatic woman, etc. and

(3) Eugenic grounds - where there is a substantial risk

that the child, if born, would suffer from deformities and diseases.[79]

Further Section 3(4) of MTPA clarifies as to whose consent would be necessary for termination of pregnancy. It states (a) No pregnancy of a woman, who has not attained the age of 18 years, or who having attained the age of 18 years, is a lunatic, shall be terminated except with the consent in writing of her guardian.[80]

An analysis of this legislation brings that woman's right in this respect is doubtful because her right is dependant on certain conditions: proof of risk to her life or grave injury to her physical or mental health, substantial risk of physical or mental abnormalities to the child if born and a situation where abortion could only save her life, all to be arrived at by the medical practitioners. Certain substantial question associated with the issue of abortion are not addressed Can a woman request a medical practitioner to perform an abortion on the ground that she does not want a child at that time? Where the liberty of the woman is fully dependant on certain other factors, such are quest cannot be said to be just and reasonable. The M.T.P. Act also does not classify the pregnancy period so that the woman's interests and the state's interests could be given predominance in one's own spheres. It is submitted that a decision as to abortion may be entirely left with woman provided she is sane and attained majority. Only in cases where an abortion may affect her life, her freedom may be curtailed. All other restrictions on the right to abortion are unwelcome. True, a woman's decision as to abortion may depend upon her physical and mental health or the potential threat to the health of the child. Apart from these reasons, there are also various important factors. She or the family may not be financially sound to welcome an addition. It may be a time when she wants to change her profession, which requires free time and hard work. Her relationship with the husband may virtually be on the verge of collapse and she may prefer not to have a child from him, for it may possibly affect the future life. All these factors are quite relevant and the Indian statute on abortion does not pay any respect to them. The law thus is unreasonable and could well be found to be violative of the principles of equality provided under Article 14 of the Constitution. Is it desirable to pay compensation to woman for all her physical and mental inconveniences and liabilities, which arises in that context. Finally it may be noted that the M.T.P. Act does not protect the unborn child. Any indirect protection it gains under the Act is only a by-product resulting from the protection of the woman. The rights provided as well as the restrictions imposed under the statute show that the very purpose of the state is to protect a living woman from dangers which may arise during an abortion process. It is the protection to the mother that protects the unborn.[81]

If we turn our attention to the judicial attitude it does not show a clear and unequivocal stand in the recent case of Niketa the arguments advanced were that in several countries, including the United Kingdom, there is no gestational age limit set for abortion in the case of foetal abnormalities Niketa's personal reason for wanting an abortion was that she did not want to give birth to a severely disabled infant and witness its suffering; the trauma caused to her and her family was an additional reason. In the case *Rajeshwari* v. *State of Tamil Nadu*[82] The case, is of an unmarried girl of 18 years who is praying for issue of a direction to terminate the pregnancy of the child in her womb, on the ground that bearing the unwanted pregnancy of the child of three months made her to become mentally ill and the continuance of pregnancy has caused great anguish in her mind, which would result in a grave injury to her mental health, since the pregnancy was caused by rape. The Court granted the permission to terminate the pregnancy.

In *Dr. Nisha Malviya and Anr.* v. *State of M.P.*[83] the accused had committed rape on minor girl aged about 12 years and made her pregnant. The allegations are that two other co-accused took this girl, and they terminated her pregnancy. So the charge on them is firstly causing miscarriage without consent of girl. The Court held all the three accused guilty of termination of pregnancy which was not consented by the mother or the girl.

Despite the Medical Termination of Pregnancy (MTP) Act in place since 1971, an estimated 4-6 million illegal abortions occur every year. While, 6-9% of these occur in adolescent girls, 16% are women between 20-34 years. These unsafe abortions also have negative consequences for women's health and seriously impact the reproductive rights of women.[84]

While some rights have been accepted as fundamental by both the international conventions as well the Indian laws, the 'Right to Health and the ensuing reproductive rights ' has yet to be acknowledged as a fundamental right in India. Women's groups, health and human rights activists in the country have been campaigning for several years for reproductive Health to be recognised as a constitutional guarantee. In this ongoing struggle, women along with these groups and activists have played a critical role in the process of formulating their health rights – in deciding what their rights should be, the content of these rights and the processes by which these rights can be claimed. These processes have also witnessed application of existing international conventions to hold the state accountable for violating these rights. The understanding and scope of women's right to health is constantly evolving as women participate more actively in these processes, causing changes in attitudes towards women and their health, bringing about change in the way laws are formulated and interpreted. Combined efforts are required now, more than ever, to demand and ensure the recognition of right to reproductive health as a fundamental right.[85]

Conclusion

The idea of reproductive rights as human rights which includes the right to found a family, the right to decide freely and responsibly the number and spacing of one's children, the right to have access to family planning information and education, and the right to have access to family planning methods and servicesis new and challenging. But consider this: Each one of us has indispensable human rights—rights that underpin our ability to live with dignity, to enjoy full and equal citizenship, to lead a healthy and fulfilling life. If a woman is to make her own decisions and live the healthiest life possible—her basic human rights—she must be able to control her reproductive life and obtain good reproductive healthcare and accurate information.

Simply put, reproductive freedom lies at the heart of the promise of human dignity, self-determination, and equality. When a woman is denied her reproductive rights—when she is denied obstetric care, birth control, the facts about reproductive health, or safe abortion, as the women above were—she is denied the means to direct her own life, protect her health, and exercise her human rights.

The right to reproductive health has clear links to many other rights. The realization of the right to reproductive health requires the fulfillment of several interconnected rights of a range of determinants, such as food, education, environment, housing, working conditions, poverty, health care and so on. Unless all these determinants are also addressed, it is not possible to ensure the right to reproductive health. The denial or enjoyment of the rights mentioned above can impact a womens ability to achieve the highest attainable standard of health, and conversely, the health status determines the enjoyment of other rights, i.e. a person who is not 'healthy' may not be able to participate fully and actively in economic, social or political activities in society.

References

1 Mumbai Abortion Case: Niketa Mehta Suffers Miscarriage, The Times of India August 14 2008.

2 SC to Hear Nari Nikeatn Rape Victim Case ,Times of India, 19 July 2009,

3 Yash Ghai, Constitutionalism and the Challenge of Ethnic Diversity, Prepared for World Justice Forum, 2008.

4 Aneikwu Nkolika Ijeoma, Engendering Sexuality: Human Rights Issues in Reproductive and Sexual Health, Presented at the 2006 ARSRC Sexuality Leadership Development Fellowship (SLDF) July 2006. Nigeria.

5 Id.

6 Tomris Trmen, "Reproductive Rights : How to Move Forward?" Health and Human Rights Vol 4 No 2, p 31, 1998.

7 The Oxford English Dictionary, Second edition, Oxford University Press.

8 World Health Organization (WHO), Safe Abortion: Technical and Policy Guidance for Health Systems 12 (2003).

9 Id.

10 Jonathan Herring ,Medical Law and Ethics, Oxford Press, p 231, 1999.

11 Aaron Wagner, "Texas Two-Step: Serving Up Fetal Rights By Side-Stepping Roe v. Wade Has Set the Table for Another Showdown on Fetal Personhood in Texas and Beyond," 32 TEX. TECH. L. REV. 1085 (2001) (discussing the return of the "fetal person" that disappeared after Roe in the vocabulary of the U.S. Congress and state lawmakers).

12 Roe, 410 U.S. at 161 observing that U.S. law has not accorded legal rights to the unborn except in the case of inheritance and tort law, and then only when the pregnancy resulted in a live birth).

13 Naral ,Pro-Choice., WHO Decides? A State-by -State Report On The Status Of Women's Reprod Rights, Nationwide Trends: 2003 in Anti-Choice And Prochoice State Legislative Activity5 (13th ed. 2004).

14 Id.

15 April L. Cherry, "A Feminist Understanding of Sex-Selective Abortion: Solely A Matter of Choice?" 10 Wis. Womens L.J. 161 (1995).

16 Id.

17 Universal Declaration of Human Rights, G.A. Res. 217A (III), U.N. GAOR, 3d Sess., at 71, U.N. Doc. A/810, 1948.

18 Id Universal declaration of Human Rights Art 25.

19 International Covenant on Economic, Social and Cultural Rights (G.A. res. 2200A (XXI), 21 U.N.GAOR Supp (No. 16) at 49, U.N. Doc. A/ 6316 (1966), 993 .N.T.S. 3, entered into force Jan. 3, 1976.

20 Id Art 12.

21 The Convention on the Rights of the Child is the first legally binding international instrument to incorporate the full range of human rights—civil, cultural, economic, political and social rights. In 1989, world leaders decided that children needed a special convention just for them because people under 18 years old often need special care and protection that adults do not.

22 Id Art 24.

23 Id Art 34.

24 UN GA Res 34/180, UN Doc A/34/46, 19 I.L.M. 33(1980).

24 Id Art 12,

25 Id.

26 Those countries that have Ratified a Covenant or a Convention and are thereby bound to conform to its provisions, available at http:// www1.umn.edu/humanrts Last visited on 4-04-2009.

27 The United Nations Committee on the Elimination of Discrimination against Women (CEDAW), an expert body established in 1982, is composed of 23 experts on women's issues from around the world. The Committee's mandate is very specific: it watches over the progress for women made in those countries that are the States parties to the 1979 Convention on the Elimination of All Forms of Discrimination against Women. A country becomes a State party by ratifying or acceding to the Convention and thereby accepting a legal obligation to counteract discrimination against women. The Committee monitors the implementation of national measures to fulfill this obligation.

28 International Convention on the Elimination of All Forms of Racial DiscriminationAdopted and opened for signature and ratification by General Assembly resolution 2106 (XX) of 21 December 1965.

29 A/CONF.171/13: Report of the ICPD (94/10/18).

30 Zelda DT Soriano, "The Impacts of Conflict on Reproductive Health and Policy Response 14 Years after ICPD" Volume 25 Number 1 September 2008.

31 Supra note 29 Chapter 7 para 7.2.

32 Id 7.3.

33 Id Paragraph 7.3.

34 Id Paragraph 7.17.

35 "Reproductive Rights In Conflict Situation" s available on http://www.wgnrr.org/docs/RSHR_Conflict.doc Last visited on 3-04-2009.

36 Fourth World Conference on Women Beijing Declaration and Plan of Action Para 93.

37 Id Para 96.

38 Id Para 94.

39 United Nations Security Council Resolution 1325 on Women, Peace and Security Art 10 Calls on all parties to armed conflict to take special measures to protect women and girls from gender-based violence, particularly rape and other forms of sexual abuse, and all other forms of violence in situations of armed conflict.

40 The Declaration was adopted by the nations of the Americas at the Ninth International Conference of American States in Bogotá, Colombia, in April 1948.

41 International Covenant on Civil and Political RightsAdopted and opened for signature, ratification and accession by General Assembly resolution 2200A (XXI) of 16 December 1966.

42 Art 2 reads Everyone's right to life shall be protected by law. No one shall be deprived of his life intentionally save in the execution of a sentence of a court following his conviction of a crime for which this penalty is provided by law.

43 (Adopted 27 June 1981, OAU Doc. CAB/LEG/67/3 rev. 5, 21 I.L.M. 58 (1982), entered intoforce 21 October 1986) Human beings are inviolable. Article 4 Every human being shall be entitled to respect for his life and the integrity of his person. No one may be arbitrarily deprived of this right.

44 World Health Organization (WHO), Safe Abortion: Technical and Policy Guidance for Health Systems 12 (2003).

45 Id.

46 "Safe and Legal Abortion is a Woman's Human Right,: Center for reproductive Rights, Briefing paper 2004.

47 Id.

48 Supra note 35 para 97 Unsafe abortions threaten the lives of a large number of women, representing a grave public health problem as it is primarily the poorest and youngest who take the highest risk. Most of these deaths, health problems and injuries are preventable through improved access to adequate health-care services, including safe and effective family planning methods and emergency obstetric care, recognizing the right of women and men to be informed and to have access to safe, effective, affordable and acceptable methods of family

planning of their choice, as well as other methods of their choice for regulation of fertility which are not against the law, and the right of access to appropriate health-care services that will enable women to go safely through pregnancy and childbirth and provide couples with the best chance of having a healthy infant.

49 Actions for the Further Implementation of the Programme of Action of the International Conference on Population and Development, U.N. GAOR, 21st Special Sess., New York, United States, June 30 - July 2, 1999, para. 63(iii), U.N. Doc. A/S-21/5/Add.1 (1999).

50 A/HRC/11/L.16/Rev.1 2009.

51 410 U.S. 113 (1973).

52 Id.

53 Ministry of Justice (United Kingdom). The UK Law statute database. Abortion Act 1967 (c.87). [cited 2008 Sep 30]. Available from: http://www.statutelaw.gov.uk/content.aspx?activeTextDocId=118107.

54 (1980) 3 EHRR 408.

55 ((1992) 73 DR 155).

56 Vo v. France, app. No. 53924/00, European Court of Human Rights, July 8, 2004, para. 85, available at http:// hudoc.echr.coe.int/hudoc/ViewRoot. Last visited on 5-05-2009.

57 Sentencia C-355/06, Constitutional Court of Colombia (2006). Cited in Women's Link Worldwide (ed.), C-355/2006: Excerpts of the Constitutional Court's Ruling that Liberalized Abortion in Colombia.

58 Id.

59 "World Abortion Policies 1999", on line, United Nations available at http://www.un.org/esa/population/publications/abt/fabt.htmLast He visited on 5-04-2009.

60 Tomris Trmen, Reproductive Rights :How To move Forward, Health and Human Rights, Vol. 4 No. 2 ,p 31.,1998.

61 WHO, The World Health Report 1999: Making a Difference (Geneva: WHO, p 98,1999).

62 VWO, "Unsafe Abortion," in Global and Regional Estimates of Incidence and Mortality Due to Unsafe Abortion, with a Listing of Available Country Data (Geneva: WHO, p1-15 1998).

63 UNAIDS, AIDS Epidemic Update (Geneva: UNAIDS, p36 1999).

64 Supra note 60.

65 WHO, Violence against Women (Geneva: WHO, p 12 ,1997).

66 http://www.infochangeindia.org/womenIbp.jsp.

67 Sama Team, 'Reproductive Health services: The Transition from Policy Discourse to Implementation' in Leena V Gangoli, Ravu Duggal and Abhay Shukla (ed) Review of Health Care in India p 166, 2005.

68 Reproductive Child Health (RCH) programme Department of Family welfare Government of India In order to effectively improve the health status of women and children and fulfil the unmet need for Family Welfare services in the country, especially the poor and under served by reducing infant child and maternal mortality and morbidity, Government of India during 1997-98 launched the RCH Programme for implementation during the 9th plan period by integrating Child Survival and Safe Motherhood (CSSM) Programme with other reproductive and child health (RCH) services.

69 Id.

70 Supra note 67.

71 Constitution of India Art 21.

72 Bandhua Mukti Morcha v. Union of India 1984 3 SCC 161.

73 Supra note 71 Art 47.

74 Indian Penal Code Section 312.

75 Medical Termination of Pregnancy Act 1971.

76 Jenna Narayan, Medical Termination Of Pregnancy Act an Archaic Society Or an Archaic society available on http://students.indlaw.com/display.aspx?4556 Last visited on 3-05-2009.

77 Id Section 3.

78 Kriti Dwivedi, Medical Termination of Pregnancy Act 1971: An overview available at http://www.legalservicesindia.com/articles/pregact.htm Last visited on 5-04-2009.

79 Supra note 74 Section 3.

80 Id Section 3(4).

81 Neha Madhiwalla, "The Niketa Mehta Case: Does the Right to Abortion Threaten Disability Rights?", Journal of Medical Ethics, Vol 4 Oct 2008.

82 1996 CrilJ 3795.

83 2000CriLJ671.

84 Kapilashrami, Anuj , Women's health: A Decade of Skewed Priorities, NGO Country Report, 2005.

85 Sarojini and others, "Women's Right to Health", National Human Right Commission.

5

Renting a Womb: Technology and Surrogacy Rights

Introduction

The intricate case of Japanese baby Manji born to an Indian surrogate mother upon fertilization of her Japanese parents' eggs and sperms in Tokyo and the embryo being implanted in Ahmedabad, triggered off complex knotty issues in India.

Japanese baby Manji Yamada was born to a surrogate Indian mother in August 2008. Her life and future was in peril since her biological intended parents divorced during pregnancy. The father applied to adopt the child, But Under, the Guardians and Wards Act, 1890, a single father cannot adopt a girl child. Further, Manji could also not be taken out of India because the legal system did not provide guidance to determine her nationality and the Japan would not issue a visa without proper documentation. The grandmother of the baby Manji, Ms Emiko Yamada flew from Japan to take care of the child and filed a petition in the Supreme Court under article 32 of the Constitution. The Court relegated her to the National Commission for Protection of Child Rights constituted under the Commissions for Protection of Child Rights Act 2005. The

Supreme Court ruled that commercial surrogacy was legal and allowed Manji to be taken out of India. This decision legally allows Manji's Father to petition to Indian authorities to rule that he is Manji's biological father. As Father, he can forgo an adoption and documents can be issued which would allow his child to enter Japan.[1] Ultimately, baby Manji left for Japan in the care of her genetic father and grandmother This case opened up a floodgate of questions and issues related to ethics and legality surrounding surrogacy. Government quickly responded by coming up with a legislation. By this legislation India became the first country to legalize commercial surrogacy.

Surrogate motherhood has such far-reaching consequences that it raises a multitude of ethical and legal questions. It has been hotly debated in courts and legislatures, and has merited consideration by Commissions, Inquiries, Working Parties and professional societies in various parts of the world.[2] This chapter critically analyses the issue of surrogacy especially from the point of view of women rights. Chapter will provide an overview of surrogacy arrangements and concepts. Further Chapter will emphasize on the International and National legislative response to this contentious issue. Chapter tries to analyze how far the surrogacy laws protect the interests of women.

Surrogacy: Historical Context

Surrogacy can be defined as "The practice whereby one woman carries a child for another with the intention that the child should be handed over after the birth.[3] In practice the child is handed over within a day of the birth.

There are two kinds of surrogacy Partial and full. In full surrogacy also known as Traditional Surrogacy or Straight or Genetic Surrogacy, Surrogate mothers eggs are fertilized with the sperm of the genetic father or of a male donor via artificial insemination.[4] In this particular category of surrogacy the surrogate is the genetic mother. This is normally the preference for couples who are finding it hard to conceive by natural means. In partial surrogacy or gestational surrogacy, the surrogate mother is not genetically related to the child. Eggs are extracted from the intended mother or egg donor and mixed with sperm from the intended father or sperm donor. The embryo will be developed in vitro beforehand. The embryos are then transferred into the surrogate's uterus. Embryos which are not transferred may be frozen and used for transfer at a later time if the first transfer does not result in pregnancy.[5] This is the option is well suited for gay and lesbian couples or of couples for whom pregnancy can be a health hazard. Gestational surrogacy can be given as only the surrogate's general health and well-being affects the child while genetic characteristics like skin, eye, and hair color do not.[6] Gestational surrogacy has become increasingly more common and presently accounts for approximately 95% of all surrogate pregnancies in the United States.[7]

Further surrogacy can be divided on the basis of monetary consideration. When surrogate receives no compensation and consideration for her pregnancy it is known as altruistic surrogacy. In normal cases even in an altruistic surrogacy expenses generally related to the pregnancy and birth such as medical expenses, maternity clothing, food etc are paid by the intended parents. As opposed to altruistic surrogacy when surrogate receives compensation and paid for her pregnancy it is known as commercial surrogacy which is legally banned in various countries and highly contentions. Commercial surrogacy is many times highly criticized and many refer it as "wombs for rent" and "outsourced pregnancies."

Despite the instinct to classify surrogacy as a modern issue, the practice of surrogacy is mentioned in the Bible. The following quote is taken from the book of Genesis: 'Abram's wife said "the Lord has restrained me from bearing children. Please go to my maid; perhaps I shall obtain children by her." Hagar bore Abram a son'.[8] Similarly, Rachel, the barren wife of Jacob, commissions her maid Bilhah to have a child by convincing Jacob to sleep with her.[9] Babylonian law and custom allowed this practice and infertile woman could use the practice to avoid the divorce which would likely otherwise be inevitable.[10]

But in modern times Noel Keane is credited with bringing surrogacy to the fore front of debates. In 1976 lawyer Noel Keane brokered the first legal agreement between a set of intended parents and a traditional surrogate mother. The surrogate mother did not receive compensation for this. This trend was picked up later and in 1980, 37-year old Elizabeth Kane, a pseudonym, made the history by giving birth as a traditional surrogate mother to a son. Her case is the first documented surrogacy arrangement that was compensated. She received $10,000 for the successful delivery of her baby. 1985 marks an important moment in the history of surrogacy. The first gestational surrogate pregnancy took place. [11]The surrogate carried the biological child of a woman who had had a hysterectomy, but had retained her ovaries. But the case that brought United States and world attention to the surrogacy occurred in 1986 and is famously known as Mary M case.[12]

Melissa Stern's conception took place under an agreement signed at Noel Keane's Infertility Center of New York on February 5, 1985. There were three parties to the agreement: Richard Whitehead gave his consent to the contract's "purposes, intents, and provisions" and to the insemination of Mary Beth Whitehead, his wife, with the sperm of William Stern. In addition, since any child born to Mary Beth Whitehead would legally be the child of her husband, he agreed that he would "surrender immediate custody of the child" and "terminate his parental rights." [13]

Mary Beth Whitehead agreed to be artificially inseminated and to form no "parent-child relationship" with the baby. She agreed that she would, upon delivery of the child, surrender her parental rights to William Stern; and she acknowledged that she would, during the term of the pregnancy, relinquish her right to make a decision about an abortion. She was permitted to seek an abortion only if the fetus was "physiologically abnormal" or if the inseminating physician agreed an abortion was required to insure her "physical health. Finally, the Whiteheads "agree[d] to assume all risks, including the risk of death, which are incidental to conception, pregnancy, [and] childbirth."[14]

Stern agreed to pay $10,000 to Whitehead. Although the $10,000 was described as "compensation for services and expenses" and the contract specifically states that the fee should "in no way be construed as a fee for termination of parental rights or a payment in exchange for consent to surrender the child for adoption.[15]

In 1986, Mary Beth Whitehead gave birth to Melissa Stern. Upon the birth of her child, Mary Beth decided she wanted to keep the baby. What followed was a long legal battle with Melissa's biological father, and intended mother, Betsy Stern, over custody, which finally ended in the Sterns getting custody, and Mary Beth getting visitation. The New Jersey Supreme Court decision prohibited additional surrogacy arrangements in that state unless "the surrogate mother volunteers, without any payment, to act as a surrogate and is given the right to change her mind and to assert her parental rights." Seventeen other states have since adopted similar guidelines.

This case elicited a divided response from feminists and scientists. Some asserted the primacy of a mother's claim to her child; others argued that any nullification of the contract would constitute a restriction upon a woman's right to control her own body. From the first documented surrogate pregnancy recorded in 1976 world of surrogacy has come along way. The amount of babies born from surrogates in the world is continuously rising. [16]

Ethical and Legal Issues

Generally discourse and debate on surrogacy centered on the adverse ethical and legal concerns arising out of it. But it has to be remembered that Surrogacy can act as a positive fore in the society. Question needs to be asked what is the basic motivation for opting to enter a surrogate arrangement. Several reasons can be advanced. Infertility is a common reason. Many points out that surrogate motherhood provide a unique prospect for certain couples to have a child biologically related to the husband. Other reasons range from the desire to avoid passing on a genetic defect to convenience. Many ethical and legal arguments can be pointed and drawn out of these draw a sharp distinction between these motivations.[17]

On the flip side many argue that surrogate arrangements depersonalize reproduction and create a separation of genetic, gestational, and social parenthood. The state sanction of surrogacy and gestational agreements with compensation will result in more of these agreements. These agreements will make the biological and genetic link more tenuous which will only weaken the biological, genetic, and sociological basis for family.[18] How surrogacy can lead to an array of legal complexities regarding motherhood was shown by *Jaycee B. v. Superior Court*[19]. A child was born to a surrogate mother using sperm and eggs from anonymous donors. The child thus had five people who could lay claim to parenthood – a genetic mother, a commissioning mother, a surrogate mother, a genetic father and a commissioning father.

Once the surrogacy is made legal there will be more gestational and surrogacy arrangements. This also indicates that more and more embryo will be utilized for this process. The remaining embryos will be destroyed. In this age where the question of granting personality status to a foetus is gaining acceptance and act as one of the impediments in the way of women's right to abortion. The practice of destruction of embryos will attract flake from many.[20] Questions also arises can informed consent ever be given by the surrogate,[21] and can anyone predict the emotions associated with relinquishing a child? World witnessed such a predicament in the Mary. M case. What are the possible adverse psychological effects on the child? What identity crisis might ensue, and will there be a desire on the part of the child to know his/her gestational mother? Will surrogate arrangements be used not only by infertile couples but also for the sake of convenience, or by single men or women? Should the surrogate be paid? Would this lead to commercialization of surrogacy and expose the surrogate mother to possible exploitation? What happens when no one wants a handicapped newborn? Should the couple and surrogate remain unknown to each other?[22] The experts are divided The Warnock Committee, the earliest formal debate on surrogacy in the UK suggested that surrogacy was a form of exploitation, suggesting that it was an unwarranted use of a person as a means to an end.[23] Because if you analyze the instances of surrogacy mostly women from poor social and economical backgrounds are exploited.

Closely linked to such ethical questions a host of legal questions arise. The major question is concerning the legal validity of the surrogacy agreements. Generally in most of the jurisdictions any contract or agreement which is opposed to public policy is void. Questions arise whether surrogacy agreements counter public policy. Assuming surrogacy to be a valid contract what happens if the surrogate decides to keep the child? [24] Can the court order the surrogate to handover the child. What would be appropriate damages for breaches of the contract? Is the question of surrogacy part of the reproductive rights of women which in turn is a fundamental right in many countries?[25]

Surrogacy and Women

"Surrogacy is a way we can give back to the world in a significant way. We're not rich people. We would never be able to donate a large sum of money for something like funding a wing of a hospital. We don't have the monetary resources to change the world. But I am able to grow big, beautiful, healthy surrogate babies. This is a way that my family can do something to change our little corner of the world, by helping another family in a way they cannot help themselves. That's what being a surrogate is about to me."[26]

Since women occupies the center stage in the entire process of surrogacy, it is important to fathom deep into her feelings, vulnerability, and rights. It is important to find out whether all or most of the surrogate mothers share the same feeling described above. A study in UK in 2002 concluded that surrogate mothers rarely had difficulty relinquishing rights to a surrogate child and that the intended mothers showed greater warmth to the child than mothers conceiving naturally. [27] Anthropological studies of surrogates have shown that surrogates engage in various distancing techniques throughout the surrogate pregnancy so as to ensure that they do not become emotionally attached to the baby. Many surrogates intentionally try to foster the development of emotional attachment between the intended mother and the surrogate child. Instead of the popular expectation that surrogates feel traumatized after relinquishment, an overwhelming majority describe feeling empowered by their surrogacy experience.[28]

In fact, quantitative and qualitative studies of surrogates over the past twenty years, mostly from a psychological or social work perspective, have confirmed that the majority of surrogates are satisfied with their surrogacy experience, do not experience "bonding" with the child they birth, and feel positively about surrogacy even a decade after the birth. Assessing such studies from a social constructionist perspective reveals that the expectation that surrogates are somehow "different" from the majority of women and that they necessarily suffer as a consequence of relinquishing the child have little basis in reality and are instead based on cultural conventions and gendered assumptions.[29] It is to be added that most of these studies were undertaken in western societies whose culture and habits widely differs from other traditional societies like India. Hence it is difficult to make a generalization regarding the wellbeing and satisfaction of surrogate mothers.

The possible discontentment's of surrogate mothers were clearly brought out by Kane, the first documented surrogate mother. Kane was completely unprepared for her feelings surrounding the birth of the surrogate baby, and though she experienced no trouble dissolving her parental rights at birth, she came to regret her decision to become a surrogate mother. Elizabeth Kane became an advocate against surrogacy; She chronicled her experiences in a book titled Birth Mother.[30] In addition to the emotional difficulties she experienced, Kane's children experienced teasing and emotional distress, the family's social positions suffered, and her husband experienced difficulties in his career. In the similar line In 1989, Whitehead published A Mother's Story: The Truth About the Baby M Case, a book about the case from her perspective. [31] In fact severing a woman's ties with a child by contract dismisses bonds between woman and child that can be created by pregnancy. A mother has a physical, psychological and social relationship with her baby during pregnancy.[32] One of the prominent ethical questions to be answered in the context of surrogacy is the concept of mother hood. A women who carries a child in the womb for nine months can the law dictate her to return the baby inspite of her wish Can the law regulate a relation between mother and child. Indian surrogates do acknowledge the psychic costs of service, including missing the children they have while confined at a clinic and missing the child they have relinquished.

Perhaps surrogacy continues to be a widely debated subject by feminists for this deeper and emotional anguish undergone by surrogate mothers. Women's movements claim that surrogate motherhood is a form of commodifying and dismembering the female body and thus a patriarchal form of violence.[33] Further they bring about and perhaps rightly various health hazards associated with surrogacy.

The literature regarding the medical risks associated with surrogate pregnancy is extremely limited. It is debatable whether obstetric risks are the same as those for any other pregnancy derived by in vitro fertilization with the same number of fetuses. Most case studies report no increase in adverse events related to surrogate pregnancy.[34] However, in one of the studies, 2 of 9 surrogate mothers underwent postpartum hysterectomy: after a delivery of triplets with placenta accrete and after uterine rupture that occurred during delivery of a macrosomic infant.[35]

Leaving aside the studies continued pregnancy affects a woman's health and one cannot completely predict and know all the long-term and short term consequences of repeated pregnancies. Studies have shown that repeated pregnancies can even affect cardiovascular health. Pregnancy can also aggravate existing health conditions and a poor uneducated woman in India and developing countries may not fully comprehend the risks, either short-term or long-term, Short-term effects range from fatigue and vomiting to the swelling of joints and the long term effects range from scarring, varicose veins to loose skin and as for complications of pregnancy, they there are many...many! [36] A baby soaks up nutrition from it's host's body and though the 'mother' might have a better diet *during* the pregnancy because of the money and care provided by the biological parents, her health may not be that good enough to begin with.[37] In India women are not as healthy as they are in the developed countries due to poorer nutrition levels since childhood. In normal surrogacy agreement the long term and short term risk associated with pregnancy is clearly missing. The agreement traditionally covers health risks only during the course of pregnancy. For instance pregnancy many times aggravate back ache what happens where four months after the delivery surrogate mother develops accuse backache which is carried life long. Question of responsibility arises in such cases.

Surrogacy agreements actually are redefining the concept of motherhood. In surrogacy who gives birth to the child is no longer presumptive mother This attempts to depersonalize the entire birth process. Compensation of women for reproductive purposes also raises the issue of exploitation.[38] Even if it is argued that surrogacy is a matter of individual choice it is always debatable whether women are choosing freely to become surrogates, or that their will is socially and economically bought. Experience suggests most of the surrogates mothers are drawn from economically and socially backward class and it is the desire for money that motivates them for surrogacy. It is for these reasons Janice G. Raymond's call surrogacy "reproductive trafficking" "because it creates a national and international traffic in women in which women become moveable property, objects of reproductive exchange, and brokered by go-betweens mainly serving the buyer.[39] Further it is always debatable whether women are choosing freely to become surrogates, or that their will is socially and economically bought or constructed."

International Legal Framework

If you analyze the international response legislative framework at the global level is missing. United Nations has not come up with a specific legislation on this topic Art 16 of Declaration of Human Rights 1948 says, inter alia, that "men and women of full age without any limitation due to race, nationality or religion have the right to marry and found a family[40]

Perhaps legislation is slow in coming because society has not yet been able to resolve the myriad of ethical and legal questions surrounding surrogate motherhood. Differing ethical and social opinions have led to legal frameworks that vary between jurisdictions. In Israel, commercial surrogacy is legal, yet familial and altruistic surrogacies are banned because of religious reasons related to incest and adultery.[41] In March 1996, the Israeli government legalized gestational surrogacy under the "Embryo Carrying Agreements Law." [42] This law made Israel the first country in the world to implement a form of state controlled surrogacy in which each and every contract must be approved directly by the state.[43] A state-appointed committee permits surrogacy arrangements to be filed only by Israeli citizens who share the same religion. Surrogates must be single, widowed or divorced and only infertile heterosexual couples are allowed to hire surrogates. [44] The numerous restrictions on surrogacy under Israeli law have prompted some intended parents to turn to surrogates outside of the country. Some turn to India because of its low costs.[45]

In the United States, surrogacy is permitted in several states with different amounts of weight given to surrogacy contracts; however, a large number of states have banned all forms of surrogacy. The Australian Capital Territory permits altruistic, but not commercial, surrogacy. Indeed, in all states in Australia, the surrogate mother is deemed by the law to be the legal mother of the child as well, and any surrogacy agreement giving custody to others is void. In addition in many states arranging commercial surrogacy is a criminal offence, although the Northern Territory has no legislation governing surrogacy at all. In the United Kingdom commercial surrogacy is not permitted.[46] In the Canada province of Quebec, any agreement whereby a woman undertakes to procreate or carry a child for another person is absolutely null. In France, since 1994, surrogacy, commercial or not is considered as unlawful and sanctioned by the law. Since 1997 ovum and sperm donation and surrogacy is legal in Georgia. According to the law a donor or surrogate mother has no parental rights over the child born. In Georgia the compensation of the surrogate mother does not exceed EUR 9 000 during the pregnancy period and after the birth of a child (post-natal rehabilitation period). The major part of the surrogate mother's compensation shall be paid after the seventeenth week of pregnancy and in the post-natal rehabilitation period.[47]

Indian Legislative and Judicial Approach

Commercial surrogacy is a booming business in India. Surrogacy is reportedly a $499-million industry in India. The low cost of the medical procedures and associated cost of surrogacy makes it a hot destination for surrogacy. [48] It was estimated that total cost of surrogacy roughly comes to around $25,000 roughly a third of the typical price in the United States.[49] The relative costs involved in the surrogacy process are probably the largest incentive for foreigners to travel to India. [50] The hot places to search these surrogate mothers are Anand and Surat of Gujarat, Indore in Madhya Pradesh and Pune in Mumbai.[51] In Anand, presently 27 Indian women are carrying the children of foreign fathers. Assisted reproductive technology has been in vogue in India since 1978, when the first in-vitro fertilisation experiment was successfully carried out. India's first gestational surrogacy took place in 1994 in Chennai. In 1997, a woman from Chandigarh, India agreed to carry a child for 50,000 rupees in order to obtain medical treatment for her paralyzed husband.[52]

If we take the legal response commercial surrogacy which is banned in some European countries and subject to a wide spectrum of regulation in U.S. states, the legal position was not clear and there was no specific law on surrogacy until recently.

The government wanted to fill this void to avoid exploitation and extortion of parties involved. In 2000, the Indian Council of Medical Research (ICMR) came out with a Statement of Specific Principles for Assisted Reproductive Technologies to check the use of assisted reproductive technology (ART) but these were non-binding provisions and often practiced neither in letter nor spirit.[53] With respect to surrogacy, the guidelines offered several protections to the surrogate:

- Surrogacy should be resorted to only when it is coupled with authorized adoption wherever applicable;
- It should be rebuttably presumed that a woman who carries the child and gives birth to it is its mother;
- The intending parents should have a preferential right to adopt the child subject to six weeks' postpartum delay for necessary maternal consent;
- The contract for surrogacy, despite permitting reasonable payment of compensation on completion of adoption, would be valid, subject to the surrogate's right to retain the baby if she so desires;
- The only remedy for the genetic parent would be to make a claim for custody on the grounds of the best interest of the child; and
- Abortion under the abortion law on medical grounds should be the inviolate right of the surrogate, and, in that event, the adopting parents have no claim over the amounts already paid.

The guideline clearly gave precedence to surrogate mothers interest by granting her legal right and giving the option to keep the baby if she so wishes. As a follow up to these guidelines and to rectify some of the drawbacks associated with the ICMR Guidelines the Secretary of Family Welfare released draft guidelines on Assisted Reproductive Technology (ART) Clinics on September 4, 2002. [54] With respect to surrogacy, the draft guidelines provided that no relative could act as a surrogate; genetic parents must adopt a child born through surrogacy; surrogacy should normally be considered only for patients for whom it would be physically or medically impossible/undesirable to carry a baby to term; and a child born through ART should be presumed to be the legitimate child of the couple, born within wedlock and with all the attendant rights of parentage, support, and inheritance.[55]

In order to regulate functioning of fertility clinics the Ministry of Health and Family Welfare published the non-binding National Guidelines for Accreditation, Supervision & Regulation of ART Clinics in India in 2005.[56] With respect to surrogacy, the Guidelines provide the following:

- The new guidelines required that "A surrogate mother carrying a child biologically unrelated to her must register as a patient in her own name. While registering she must mention that she is a surrogate mother and provide all the necessary information about the genetic parents such as names, addresses, etc. She must not use/register in the name of the person for whom she is carrying the child, as this would pose legal issues.[57] In Hyderabad the doctor-in-charge, totally on humanitarian an grounds, agreed to register a woman who was acting as a surrogate for her sister, in her sister's name. After the registration and examination of the patient, the doctor realized that there would be a problem if the woman does not survive the delivery. Whose death certificate would the doctor sign?[58]
- "The birth certificate shall be in the name of the genetic parents. The clinic, however, must also provide a certificate to the genetic parents giving the name and address of the surrogate mother."[59]
- "All the expenses of the surrogate mother during the period of pregnancy and post-natal care relating to pregnancy should be borne by the couple seeking surrogacy. The surrogate mother would also be entitled to monetary compensation from the couple for agreeing to act as a surrogate; the exact value of this compensation should be decided by discussion between the parties[60] Compensation negotiations between a couple and the surrogate mother must be conducted independently between them."[61] "An [egg] donor cannot act as a surrogate mother for the couple to whom the [egg] is

being donated."[62]

- Consent must be true informed consent and must be witnessed by one who is not associated with the clinic.[63]
- "Payments to surrogate mothers should cover all genuine expenses associated with the pregnancy. Documentary evidence of the financial arrangement for surrogacy must be available. The ART center should not be involved in this monetary aspect." [64]
- "Advertisements regarding surrogacy should not be made by the ART clinic. The responsibility of finding a surrogate mother, through advertisement or otherwise, should rest with the couple, or a semen bank."

Realizing the drawbacks and Forced by the developments in the case of Japanese Baby Manji Government has come up with a comprehensive legislation on assisted reproductive technologies. The Bill has been drafted by the Ministry of Health and Family Welfare, along with the Indian Council for Medical Research (ICMR).[65]

Assisted Reproductive Technology Act 2008

The new Assisted Reproductive Technology (Regulation) Bill & Rules, 2008, legalises commercial surrogacy, stating that both the couple or individual seeking surrogacy through the use of assisted reproductive technology, and the surrogate mother, shall enter into a surrogacy agreement which shall be legally enforceable.[66] For the implementation and overseeing the provisions of the Act it envisages the establishment of a Board to be known as the National Advisory Board for Assisted Reproductive Technology. The surrogate mother may receive monetary compensation for carrying the child in addition to health-care and treatment expenses during pregnancy. [67] The document puts certain obligation on the surrogate mother The surrogate mother will relinquish all parental rights over the child once the amount is transferred and birth certificates will be in the name of genetic parents.[68] The prescribed age-limit for a surrogate mother is between 21- 45 years.[69] The Bill also states that no surrogate mother can undergo an embryo transfer more than three times for the same couple. The document also envisages that woman seeking or agreeing to act as a surrogate mother shall be medically tested for such diseases, sexually transmitted or otherwise, as may be prescribed, and all other communicable diseases which may endanger the health of the child, and must declare in writing that she has not undergone intravenous medical treatment or received a blood transfusion.[70]

Single parents can also have children using a surrogate mother.[71] All foreigners seeking infertility treatment in India will first have to register with their embassy. Their notarised statement will then have been handed over to the treating doctor. The foreign couple will also state whom the child should be entrusted to in case of an eventuality such as a genetic parent's. The bill also includes opportunities for unmarried individuals or couples to have their own children through artificial insemination with donor sperm (AID).

The Bill is inadequate in protecting and safeguarding the rights and health of the women who undergo these procedures, surrogates and egg donors and of the children born through these techniques. The Bill actively promotes medical tourism in India for reproductive purposes. Though the Bill takes some step to regulate the process of surrogacy in the context of growing numbers of foreign couples coming to India, the equally important issue of Indian women also becoming egg 'donors` for foreign couples is not taken into consideration.[72]

The Bill denies the critical developmental needs of the baby and provides that baby be handed over to the parents fast. This is done in order to make separation easy and quick for a commercial surrogate, ensures fast separation. This is against certain basic interests of the child.At the same time one positive aspect of the legislation is its clarification on the rights of child. The document envisages that A child may, upon reaching the age of 18, apply for any information, relating to his / her genetic parent or parents or surrogate mother. But this does not applicable to personal information. This in consonance with Article 7-1 of the UN Convention on the Rights of the Child (CRC) recognises 'as far as possible, the right to know and be cared for his parents'. [73] Further on Similar lines European Court of Ha child as aright to know of its parentage in the case of *Gaskin* v. *United Kingdom.*[74] The same right has been conferred on the he legal guardian of a minor child who may apply for any information, excluding personal identification, about his / her genetic parent or parents or surrogate mother when required, and to the extent necessary, for the welfare of the child. The document further clarifies that personal Personal identification of the genetic parent or parents or surrogate mother may be released only in cases of life threatening medical conditions which require physical testing or samples of the genetic parent or parents or surrogate mother. Provided that such personal identification will not be released without the prior informed consent of the genetic parent or parents or surrogate.[75] This is a positive measure and should be remembered that the child in the baby M case Melissa Stern when she reached age 18, she went to court to terminate Mary Beth Whitehead's maternal rights and to formalize Elizabeth Stern's parenthood through adoption.

Further it puts certain serious handicaps on women neglecting her health hazards. It bans the donation of ova by her. It goes to the extent of permitting three surrogate births to a woman and three cycles of ova transfer for a single couple without any reference to the health risks to the surrogate. This takes the number of times she can undergo IVF cycles to a high figure, thus jeopardising her physical and mental health. Along similar lines, the Bill permits a woman to donate her eggs six times in her life, at intervals of three months, which again could be hazardous for her health. But an important aspect of the maximum number of eggs that can be retrieved in each IVF cycle is still left untouched in the legislation, thereby completely leaving it in the hands of the providers to decide on this.

At the same time the right to demand abortion and pregnancy reduction is given to the commissioning parents and the surrogate is bound to oblige. This is against a womens right to abortion which is widely accepted as part of the reproductive rights of women and is considered as part of fundamental rights. No attention is paid to the right of the surrogate to keep the baby if she changes her mind early or due to the death of her own child.[76] The question arises can a women be forced to carry pregnancy against her wish. This is a very regressive measure as such no science can predict the emotion which a woman may develop after the birth of a baby. This provision following a contractual agreement may appears o be perfectly in consonance with law but against the basic principles of motherhood.

The Bill, making commercial surrogacy legal, prohibits the use of the egg of the surrogate mother for attaining pregnancy. This implies that an infertile couple will have to look for a surrogate as well as an egg donor; further, a woman with a healthy reproductive system (surrogate) will be subjected to a complicated, hazardous and expensive procedure like in vitro fertilisation rather than a simpler one like intra uterine insemination (IUI). The legislation is self-contradictory when it comes to protecting the anonymity of the surrogate. Sec 34(11) provides that Subject to the provisions of this Act, all information about the surrogate shall be kept confidential and information about the surrogacy shall not be disclosed to anyone other than the central database of the Indian Council of Medical Research, except by an order of a court of competent jurisdiction. Further clause (14) of Sec 34 imposes duty on assisted reproductive technology clinic not to disclose information on or about surrogate mothers or potential surrogate mothers to any person. But in contradiction Sec 34(8) provides that "A surrogate mother shall, in respect of all medical treatments or procedures in to the concerned child, register at the hospital or such medical facility in her own name, clearly declare herself to be a surrogate mother, and provide the name or names and addresses of the person or persons, as the case may be, for whom she is acting as a surrogate, along with a copy of the certificate mentioned in clause 17" If the legislation makes it mandatory for the surrogate to disclose her identity, then it is unclear as to how her privacy and anonymity will be maintained. [77]

The Bill mandates the appointment of a local guardian in case of foreign couples. The purpose of appointing local guardian is to take care of the surrogate during the gestation period till the child is delivered to the foreigner or foreigner couple. But the problem with the bill is that it does not specify who can be appointed as local guardian and what should be his or her qualification.

The person or persons who have availed of the services of a surrogate mother shall be legally bound to accept the custody of the child / children irrespective of any abnormality that the child / children may have, and the refusal to do so shall constitute an offence under this Act. The legal parentage of children born through surrogacy has not been adequately tackled and situations where the intended couple no longer want the child, split up, pass away or abandon the child have not been addressed. After reaching an agreement, if the childless parents die, what will happen to the surrogate mother Who will take the responsibility, if the foreign parents never come back to get their child The legislation also clarifies that the name on the birth certificate will be that of the genetic parents, thus equating the term with intended parents/parent. Such a clause, although protecting the anonymity of the donor, presumes that the intended parents will also be the genetic parents.

The document is still ambiguous on certain key areas like the maximum age of women who can opt for ARTs (while mentioning the minimum age to be 21 years), the eligibility of persons from different sexual orientations for accessing these technologies, and listing the disorders/diseases that a gamete donor and surrogate need to be screened for. Certain other clauses also call for an explanation of the rationale behind them, like prohibiting the use of sperm or eggs from a relative or a known person, prohibition of genetic surrogacy, and the role envisaged for the semen banks. The Bill is weak on the operational realities of the processes it aims to put in place and contradicts itself at several places. [78]

But drawbacks include possible commercialization and exploitation. Additionally, the provision that family member surrogates have to belong to the same generation will lead to problems for many. "What about cases where an aunt, aged 30 is perfectly health and willing to be the surrogate for her 20-year-old niece. For instance in 2004, there was a case in India where a mother aged 43 had been the surrogate for her daughter.

Some women activists say the bill has overlooked serious issues – for instance, the bill does not state the minimum remuneration that a surrogate mother should receive.They further argue that Surrogacy turns a normal biological function of a woman's body into a commercial contract. Surrogate services are advertised. Surrogates are recruited and operating agencies make large profits. The commercialism of surrogacy raises fears of black market and baby selling, breeding farms, turning impoverished women into baby producers and the possibility of selective breeding at a price. Surrogacy degrades a pregnancy to a service and a baby to a product.[79]

Any discussion on surrogacy will not be complete without the mention of fundamental rights under constitution. Question arises whether surrogacy agreements can stand the scrutiny of fundamental rights. The articles relevant to discussion here relates to Fundamental Rights provisions, The relevant fundamental rights which can be said to have some connection with the issues and legal questions arising out of surrogacy is

Article 21. Which guarantees "protection of life" as a fundamental right and reads: "No person shall be deprived of life or personal liberty except according to procedure established by law."[80] The courts in India have always used this provision to emphasize the dignity of individual. The Judiciary in India too has recognized the reproductive right of humans as a basic right. For instance, in *B. K. Parthasarthi v. Government of Andhra Pradesh*[81], the Andhra Pradesh High Court upheld "the right of reproductive autonomy" of an individual as a facet of his "right to privacy" and agreed with the decision of the US Supreme Court in *Jack T. Skinner v. State of Oklahoma*[82], which characterised the right to reproduce as "one of the basic civil rights of man"

The question arises whether surrogacy agreement and process can be violative of Article 21. There are two issues to be decided. Whether surrogacy process in itself violates human dignity and brings commoditization. Human Dignity is the basis of all fundamental rights. Further the ART bill 2008 does not confer the right to abortion on surrogate. Though Indian court has never ruled right to abortion to be part of Art 21, it has to be mentioned that India is part of various Human right treaties and convention including Convention on the Elimination of All Forms of Discrimination Against Women (CEDAW).[83] These convention positively interpret the right to abortion as part of the reproductive rights. Further some critics has equated surrogacy to bonded labour and trafficking. It is to be seen whether Supreme Court will resort to Art 23 to determine various aspect of surrogacy. One of the major arguments which critics may take against commercial surrogacy relates to the technologies of human organ donation and of surrogacy. They point out that there is no need to treat both these differently. Human organ donation is restricted to a non-commercial transaction by the Human Organ Transplant Act, 1994.[84] However, temporary lending of uterus on payment has not been objected to by the state. This irrational distinction between human body parts donated and those rented does not have a co-relation.

In this regard the recommendation of the Law Commission is note worthy. It noted that the legal issues related with surrogacy are very complex and need to be addressed by a comprehensive legislation. Surrogacy involves conflict of various interests and has inscrutable impact on the primary unit of society viz. family. Non-intervention of law in this knotty issue will not be proper at a time when law is to act as ardent defender of human liberty and an instrument of distribution of positive entitlements. At the same time, prohibition on vague moral grounds without a proper assessment of social ends and purposes which surrogacy can serve would be irrational. Active legislative intervention is required to facilitate correct uses of the new technology i.e. ART and relinquish the cocooned approach to legalization of surrogacy adopted hitherto. The need of the hour is to adopt a pragmatic approach by legalizing altruistic surrogacy arrangements and prohibit commercial ones.[85] The recommendation conflict with the provision s of the bill which makes commercial surrogacy legal. It is submitted that the recommendations of law commission fails to acknowledge the ground realities.

Conclusion

Surrogacy continues to be a complicated tangle of legal, social, ethical and technological issues. Expert's points out that surrogacy fulfill an important biological and emotional and social need: This is a gift to those couples who does not or cannot have a baby of their own. Further by legalizing surrogacy Government as only recognized and acknowledged the existing state of affairs in India.

It can not always be calculated that all surrogacy agreements are against human rights and will lead to abuses. What is the need of the hour is to regulate surrogacy and make sure that it does not lead to pure commercialization, convenience and exploitation of abject poverty of people. Many of the scientific and emotional aspects of surrogacy is not known. For instance science has proved that a child in the womb is greatly influenced by the internal and external factors. Science even point that the learning process and emotional developments starts in the womb itself. Many on surrogacy highlight the distance techniques used by surrogates to distance themselves from the child Question arises will this entire process influences the future development of child. Many More research needs to be undertaken. It may be worthwhile to draw an analogy between surrogacy and international adoption. The welfare of children has always received the highest priority from both the legislative and judicial approach. The similar approach should be replicated in the sensitive case of surrogacy also where the question of thousands of women's human rights are at stake.

References

1 "Baby Born to Surrogate Indian Mother, Japanese Father allowed to leave India", MAINICHI DAILY NEWS, Oct. 18, 2008, available at < http://mdn.mainichi.jp/mdnnews/news/20081018p2a00m0na004000c.html;>Last visited on 5-06-2009. Also see "Japan gate-pass for baby Manji", The Telegraph, Oct. 18, 2008, http://www.telegraphindia.com/1081018/jsp/nation/story_9984517.jsp Last visited on 5-06-2009.

2 Sue A. Meinke, "Surrogate Motherhood: Ethical and Legal Issues", Scope Note 6, National Reference Center for Bioethics Literature, Washington.

3 Warnock Report, Para 8.1, 1984,U.K.

4 Sue Austin, "Types of Surrogacy Options in Medical Tourism" available at <httt://ezinearticles.com/?Types-of-Surrogacy-Options-in-Medical-Tourism&id=1076038>Last visited on 7-04-20090.

5 Jenn Z., Definition and Types of Surrogacy, available at <http://www.surromomsonline.com/articles/define.htm>Last visited on (10-03-2009).

6 Supra note 4 See Austin Jamie Sue Austin.

7 Judith F. Daar, "Reproductive Technologies and the Law", 426 (2006).

8 Dr Rebecca Gibbs, "Surrogacy: Medical, Ethical and Legal Issues to be Considered", North East Essex, 2006.

9 See Genesis 30:1-8.

10 J.N. Postgate, J.N.. Early Mesopotamia Society and Economy at the Dawn of History. Routledge. p. 105., (1992).

11 W H Utian , "Successful Pregnancy After an In-vitro Fertilization-Embryo Transfer from an Infertile Woman to a Surrogate", 313 New Eng. J. Med. 1351 (1985).

12 In re Baby M, 537 A.2d 1227 (N.J. 1988).

13 Id.

14 Id.

15 Id.

16 Id.

17 Supra note 4.

18 Id.

19 42 Cal.App.4Th 718 (1996).

20 Surrogacy and Gestational Agreements, Guide to the Issues available on http://www.mfc.org/legmanual/marriage%204.pdf last visited on 3-04-2009.

21 SAMA Team, Assisted Reproductive Technologies in India: Implications for Women, 42 Econ. & Pol. Wkly. 2184 (2007) (In a study of 23 ART providers in India, only one provider was found to be using informed consent forms in English as well as the local language. Patients reported trouble understanding the doctor because he or she often spoke in English only, and they feared offending the physician by requesting more information.

22 Id.

23 Den van Akker O.B.A., Organizational Selection and Asessment of Women Entering a Surrogacy agreement in the UK. Human Reproduction Vol. 14, No. 1, 262-266, (1999).

24 Dyer C., "Surrogate Mother Refuses to Give up Baby". BMJ, 314:247, (1997).

25 In Roe v. Wade Supreme Court of USA declared reproductive rights to be part of a womens fundamental rights.

26 <http://www.information-on-surrogacy.com/being-a-surrogate.html> Last visited on 5-06-2009.

27 MacCallum, F. "Surrogacy: The Experience of Commissioning Couples Human Reproduction". A study by the Family and Child Psychology Research Centre at City University, London, 87 (2003).

28 Ragone, H. Surrogate Motherhood: Conception in the Heart. West

view Books., p 45 (2001).

29 Id.

30 Kane Elizabeth, Birth Mother, Sun Books, 1990.

31 Mary Witehead, A Mother's Story: The Truth About the Baby M Case, St Martins, 1989.

32 Randy Frances Kandel, "Which Came First: The Mother or the Egg? A Kinship Solution to Gestational Surrogacy," 47 RUTGERS L. REV. 165, 187 (1994).

33 Andy Pu'cã, Controversial issues of Maternity Substitution, available at http://eirp2009.univ-danubius.ro/proceedings/pdf/1sj/4dp/3.pdf (Last visited on 5-06-2009).

34 Corson SL, Kelly M, Braveman AM. "Gestational Carrier Pregnancy. ":670-4.,(1989),

35 Duffy DA, Nulsen JC, Maier DB, . Obstetrical Complications in Gestational Carrier Pregnancies. Fertil Steril 83:749-54,(2005).

36 Surrogacy in India Problems and Laws available at http://nitawriter.wordpress.com/2007/11/01/surrogacy-law-to-be-drafted-in-india-at-long-last/Last viisted on 4-06-2009.

37 Evans, J., Playing God? Human Genetic Engineering and the Rationalization of Public Biothical Debate. Chicago: University of Chocago Press,(2002).

38 Id.

39 G. Raymond, Reproduction, Population, Technology and Rights, Women In Action (1998), available at http://www.isiswomen.org/wia/wia298/rep00001.html.

40 Universal Declaration on Human Rights 1948.

41 Dan R. Reilly, Surrogate Pregnancy: a Guide for Canadian Prenatal Healthcare Providers, CMAJ 176(4) 483, February 13, 2007.

42 Embryo Carrying Agreements Law 1996.

43 Teman, Elly. "The Last Outpost of the Nuclear Family: A Cultural Critique of Israeli Surrogacy Policy," forthcoming in: Birenbaum-Carmeli, Daphna and Yoram Carmeli (eds.), Kin, Gene, Community: Reproductive Technology among Jewish Israelis, Oxford: Berghahn Books, 2002.

44 Weisberg, K. The Birth of Surrogacy. Florida: University of Florida Press, p 210 (2005).

45 Supra note 33.

46 In the United Kingdom, Legislation on Surrogacy, the Surrogacy

Arrangements Act of 1985, was rushed through as a result of the Baby Cotton case.

47 Surrogate Motherhood Center of Georgia, available on http:// www.surrogacy.ge/last visited on 4-05-2009).

48 Jennifer L. Watson, Note, Growing a Baby for Sale or Merely Renting a Womb: Should Surrogate Mothers be Compensated for Their Services?, 6 Whittier J. Child & Family Advoc. 529, 551 (2007).

49 Amelia Gentleman, Foreign Couples Turn to India for Surrogate Mothers:, New York times, March 4, 2008 available at <http:// www.iht.com/articles/2008/03/04/asia/mother.php, Last visited on -05-2009).

50 Abigail Haworth, Surrogate Mothers: Womb for Rent, available at <http://www.marieclaire.com/world/articles/surrogate-mothers-india> (last visited Oct. 31, 2008).

51 Sujit Roy, Surrogate Mother hood :Should it be allowed, available at <http://www.merinews.com/catFull.jsp?articleID=136765>Last visited on 6-05-2009>.

52 Sandhya Srinivasan, "Surrogacy Comes Out of the Close"t, Sunday Times Of India A, July 6, ,p1 (1997).

53 Indian Council of Med. Res., Ethical Guidelines for Biomedical Research on Human Subjects 97 (2000), available at http:// www.icmr.nic.in/ethical_guidelines.pdf.Last viisted on 5-04-2009.

54 Ministry of Health & Family Welfare, Guidelines on Assisted Reproductive Technology Clinics in India (Sept. 4, 2002), available at http://pib.nic.in/archieve/lreleng/lyr2002/rsep2002/04092002/ r040920029.htmLast visited on 8-03-2009.

55 Id.

56 Indian Council of Medical Research, National Academy of Medical Sciences (India). National guidelines for accreditation, supervision and regulation of ART clinics in India. New Delhi: Ministry of health and family welfare, government of India; 2005.

57 Id. Sec. 3.4.8.

58 Pushpa M. Bhargava, The Social, Moral, Ethical, Legal and Political Implications of Today's Biological Technologies: An Indian Point of View, Biotechnol. J. 1, 34–46,(2006).

59 Supra note 56 Sec 3.5.4.

60 Id.

61 Id Sec3.9.2.

62 Ibid.

63 Id. Sec 3.5.22.

64 Id 3.10.3.

65 The Assisted Reproductive Technology (Regulation) Bill, 2008.

66 Id Sec Art 34(1).

67 Id, Section 34(2 &3) 2) All expenses, including those related to insurance, of the surrogate related to a pregnancy achieved in furtherance of assisted reproductive technology shall, during the period of pregnancy and after delivery as per medical advice, and till the child is ready to be delivered as per medical advice, to the biological parent or parents, shall be borne by the couple or individual seeking surrogacy. (3) Notwithstanding anything contained in sub-section (2) of this section and subject to the surrogacy agreement, the surrogate mother may also receive monetary compensation from the couple or individual, as the case may be, for agreeing to act as such surrogate.

68 Id, Section 34 (4) No woman under twenty one years of age and over forty five years of age shall be eligible to act as a surrogate mother under this Act.

69 Id, Section 34 (5) " no woman shall act as a surrogate for more than three successful live births in her life."

70 Id Art 34(8).

71 Id section 34 (7).

72 Sarojini N B, Aastha Sharma, The Draft ART (Regulation) Bill: in Whose Interest? Indian Journal of Medical Ethics Jan–Mar 2009.

73 The delegations of the United States and Germany insisted upon the insertion of the words 'as far as possible' in response to the original draft submitted by a few Muslim countries. UN Doc. E/CN.4.1989/48, 18-22. For a commentary on the UN Children's Right Convention, see in particular: S. Detrick, A Commentary on the United Nations Convention on the Rights of the Child, 1999.

74 Gaskin v. United Kingdom, Appl. no. 10454/83, 7 July 1989.

75 Id.

76 Imrana Qadeer, "Social and Ethical Basis of Legislation on Surrogacy: Need for Debate", Indian J Med Ethic, Jan-Mar;6(1).2009.

77 Supra note 72.

78 Supra note 72 See Sarojini.

79 Malini Karkal, "Srrogacy from a Feminist Perspective" Med Ethics. Oct-Dec;5(4),(1997).

80 Constitution Of India Art 21.

81 AIR 2000 A. P. 156.

82 316 US 535.

83 UN GA Res 34/180, UN Doc A/34/46, 19 I.L.M. 33(1980).

84 Transplantation of Human Organ Act 1994, provides If any donor had, in writing and in the presence of two or more witnesses (at least one of whom is a near relative of such person), unequivocally authorised at any time before his death, the removal of any human organ of his body, after his death, for therapeutic purposes, the person lawfully in possession of the dead body of the donor shall, unless he has any reason to believe that the donor had subsequently revoked the authority aforesaid, grant to a registered medical practitioner all reasonable facilities for the removal, for therapeutic purposes, of that human organ from the dead body of the donor.

85 Need for Legislation to Regulate Assisted Reproductive Technology Clinics as well as Rights and Obligations of Parties to a Surrogacy, Law Commmission of India 228, 2009.

6

Climate Change and Impact on Women: Need for a New Legal Paradigm

"There will be no climate justice without gender justice"

Introduction

Climate Change is one of the most significant global environmental, economic and social challenges, with considerable consequences for food security, livelihood water supply, health, energy, etc. Climate Change and ensuing consequences are not local but all pervasive. Although the hazards associated with Climate Change impact societies all over the world, it is important to recognize that they have a different effect on men and women, ethnic groups, social classes, age groups, etc. Despite the importance of recognizing gender-related differences, both the United Nations Framework Convention on Climate Change and Kyoto Protocol fail to recognize the gender differences in climate change. The Chapter discusses the impact of Climate Change with special reference to women. Chapter further looks at the possibilities and limitations of the role of women in mitigating Climate Change. The chapter critically analyzes the various legislative and policy options initiated to combat Climate change and will analyze whether gender concerns finds a place in it. Chapter strongly brings out a case for making climate change discourse more gender sensitive.

Climate Change and Impact on humanity

The world's climate system is under constant change.[1] However, scientists have shown that a byproduct of the industrialization in the last centuries has been a rapid and drastic shift in the composition of gases constituting the atmosphere, leading to the phenomenon known as global warming The rapid manner at which climate change is taking place that it is recognized as the greatest challenge for societies in the twenty first century.[2] Long-standing interpretations and observations substantiate that our climate is indeed undergoing a change at a rapid rate as a result of global warming. The scientific evidences further indicate that the warming and change in the 21st century will be significantly greater than in the 20th century.

Various research studies have thrown enough light on the possible impacts of climate change. Some of the obvious effects of climate change are already observed. Inter governmental Panel on Climate Change (IPCC) released its Fourth Assessment Report, stating "with very high confidence the global average net effect of human activities since 1750 has been one of warming."[3] The report is regarded as the consensus on the anthropogenic influence on climate change.[4] Besides Stern report stressed that "It is crucial to underline here that the effects of climate change will be distributed unevenly around the world. Whereas few developed countries can feel some benefits depending on the scale of global warming, the poorest nations will experience extremely adverse effects almost immediately."[5]

Some of the obvious effects of climate change consists of coastal erosion, Air and water pollution, habitat fragmentation, wetland loss, and reductions in fisheries, agricultural production loss of livelihood etc. It is to be noted that all effects of climate change can not be predicted with certainty there is bound to be some unforeseen and unanticipated changes. Most of these unpredictability arises because of the complex interrelation between climate, environmental stresses, and socio economic alteration. Thus these anticipated and unanticipated "surprises" may stem from unforeseen changes in the physical climate system, such as major alterations in ocean circulation, cloud distribution, or storms; and unpredicted biological consequences of these physical climate changes, such as massive dislocations of species or pest outbreaks. In addition, unexpected social or economic changes, including major shifts in prosperity, technology, or political priorities, could affect our ability to respond to climate change.[6] Regarding Social structure, the position and status of women in terms of their access to resources, decision making capacity, mobility etc plays a major role and are social factors that interact with and alter sensitivity to climate variability and change.

The impacts associated to Climate Change vary from one country to another, from one region to another, and within the same community it can have varying degrees of effect. In the words of IPCC "Although climate chan-ge impacts will affect all countries, its impacts will be differently distributed among different regions, generations, age classes, income groups, occupations and genders" [7] Generally the poorest populations and marginal groups, like children, women, and aged suffer the most brunt of climate change or any natural or artificial disasters as a consequence of their social roles.[8] It is predicted that women, principally in developing countries, will be disproportionately and excessively affected [9] Women are predominantly vulnerable to climate change because they are more prone to the adverse impacts from climate change.

Assuming continued growth in world greenhouse gas emissions a wider range of outcomes is possible with differing impacts on women. Temperature increases which will vary from one region to the next. Heavy and extreme precipitation events are likely to become more frequent, yet some regions will get drier.[10] One of the most anticipated consequences may be a rise in sea level. As sea levels rise, the livelihoods of people living in low-lying coastal zones are threatened, flooding levels increase, erosion is accelerated, wetlands and mangroves are threatened, and seawater intrudes into freshwater resources. Climate change and the resulting rise in sea level are likely to exacerbate threats to buildings, roads, powerlines, and other infrastructure in climatically sensitive places. [11]

Vulnerability of Women

Threat to Ecosystems

Many ecosystems are highly vulnerable to the magnitude of climate change. Due to change in climate ,changes in the structure of ecosystems, alteration in the geographic range of species, growing risk of extinction of up to 30% of animal and plant species is predicted. Loss of wild ancestors of food, medicinal plants, and reduction in wooded cover is also expected. This will adversely affect access to various basic needs and natural resources, such as shelter, food, fertile land, water and fuel becomes hampered. The precious flora and fauna lost through the disappearance or fragmentation of certain ecosystems are likely to be costly or impossible to replace. Women's responsibilities and role in the family set up make them more vulnerable to climate change and ensuing threat to ecosystems. They find their workload increases in their multiple roles as food producers and providers, as guardians of health, care givers, and economic actor, and educators .[12]

Food security

The Convention on Biological Diversity (CBD) points out that agricultural ecosystems and food security are especially vulnerable to climate change.[13] Climate change is predicted to reduce crop yields and food production in various regions, particularly the tropics. Traditional food sources may become more unpredictable and scarce as the climate changes. For instance Maize, sorghum, millet and groundnut yields have a strong association with the year-to-year variability of El Niño/ Southern Oscillation in Africa. For southern Africa the productivity is expected to drop by 20–50% in extreme El Niño years. If global climate changes move more towards El Niño-like conditions, crop production in Africa will decline.[14] These impacts put strain on limited resources and settlements.[15] For instance with a reduction in crop production managing domestic animals like cattle, sheep, goats, pigs, and poultry for livelihood also get affected.

Women are the main producers of the world's staple crops, providing up to 90% of the rural poor's food intake and producing 60–80% of the food in most developing coun-tries Specifically they are responsible for 70–80 percent of household food production in sub-Saharan Africa, 65 percent in Asia, and 45 percent in Latin America and the Caribbean. They achieve this despite unequal access to land, information, and inputs such as improved seeds and fertilizer. Decreased Crop production could increase their difficulty in accessing resources, hence, creating an increased workload for women who has to lookout for alternatives to maintain family. This will in turn effect the gendered division of labour, and possibly have negative effects on both men's and women's incomes. Women's informal rights to resources could decrease or disappear as access to natural resources diminishes due to climate change. [16] Women's livelihoods are affected and as a result women slip deeper in poverty, leading to more inequality and marginalization.

Water

Climate change may exacerbate existing shortages of water. Women, largely responsible for water collection in their communities, are more sensitive to the changes in seasons and climatic conditions that affect water quantity and accessibility that make its collection even more time-consuming.

It should be remembered that because of gender discrimination, women and girls face extreme burdens in times of food shortages and water scarcity. Women including pregnant and nursing women, who have the greatest need for nutritious food—tend to eat last and least when food is scarce. Moreover, as the time-consuming and labor intensive task of gathering and transporting water generally falls to women, their workload increases dramatically when water becomes scarce. One result of this increased burden is that girls' school enrollment drops as they trek longer distances to find water.[17] These possible changes in the workload suggest that climate change increase women's responsibilities in the domestic scene, in many paid and unpaid workplaces

Health

Climate change has a predominant effect on human health. Decreased drinking water availability and threatening food security due to reduced agricultural production and destruction of crops put a severe strain on human health resulting in increased malnutrition, diarrhoea, and cardiorespiratory diseases. In order to make matters worse increased global warming brings along a host of associated stress and respiratory illness. The question often arises how does this situation has a peculiar negative effect on women than men. In most of the societies women play the role of primary care givers. Women may see their responsibilities increase as family members suffer increased illness. Further, in the developing world, women often have less access to medical care than men.[18]

Migration

Due to shortage of resources male out-migration may become a recurrent phenomenon This outer migration will put more burden and increased work for women since women have to not only take care of domestic cores and rest of family members but tackle outside pressure too. Many times the shortage of resources force all out migration and relocation of people. The effects it has on women's autonomy can be complex and questionable. Relocation put severe impact on social and ecological support networks and family ties of women. Further studies have proved that migration causes conflicts over resources and conflicts cause more violence against women.[19]

Fishing

About 35 million people worldwide depend on fishing and aquaculture, including a substantial number of women [20] If the GHG emissions scenario remains as present, climate warming could result in biannual thermal stress spells causing coral bleaching.[21] This phenomenon could result in the loss of a key marine ecosystem that supports many marine resources essential to women's livelihoods including their fishing and tourism activities.[22] Changes in fish communi-ties can have a severe impact on fisherwomen.

Disaster

Women and children are 14 times more likely to die than men during a any disaster. In the 1991 cyclone disaster which killed 140,000 in Bangladesh, 90% of victims were women.[23] Similarly in industrialized countries, more women than men died during the 2003 European heat wave.[24] During Hurricane Katrina in the USA, African-American women who were the poorest population in that part of the country faced the greatest obstacles to survival.[25] Empirical evidence shows that they suffer a greater impact in a disaster or emergency; and economic losses have a disproportionate effect on economically vulnerable women .[26] In the post-disaster stage there may also be high levels of violence against women.[27]

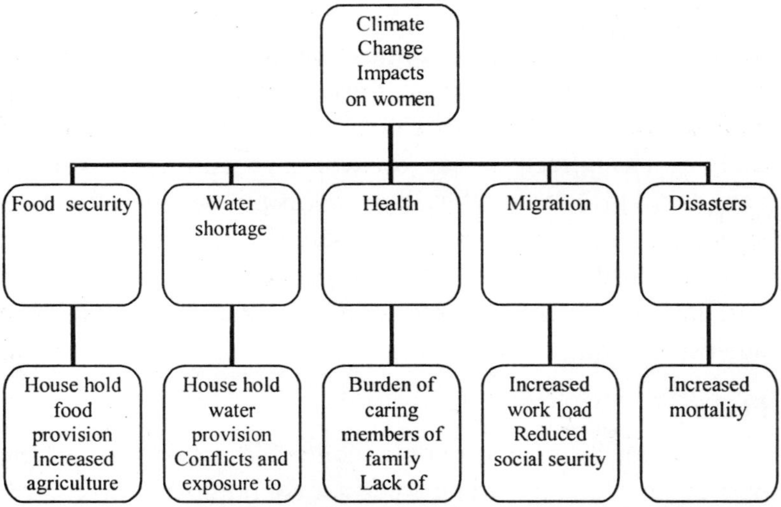

Fig. 1. Special vulnerabilities of women as a result of climate change

In short women are more strongly affected by the effects of Climate change.[28] Climate Change magnifies existing inequalities. Apart from physical and material losses, climate change results in major psychosocial issues as well. Women's low social status as a result of poverty, lack of assets, lack of education, and unequal access to information makes it imperative. To make matters worse women are often most invisible in Climate Change mitigation and adaptation policies and straytegies.The structures and the patriarchal ideology on which the climate change discourse takes place have led to women's invisibility.[29]

Significant uncertainties remain in the science underlying climate changes and their impacts. Further research would improve understanding and our ability to project societal and ecosystem impacts. However; it is likely that some aspects and impacts of climate change will be totally unanticipated as complex systems respond to ongoing climate change in unforeseeable ways.[30] Climate change does not affect women and men in the same way and it has, and will have, a gender-differentiated impact. Therefore all aspects related to climate change i.e. mitigation, adaptation, policy development, decision making) must include a gender perspective.[31]

India and Climate Change

Currently, India is ranked as one of the top five emitters of greenhouse gas emissions,[32] but as a developing country whose industrial activity and development began in the later half of the 20th century it does not bear historical responsibility for climate changes. Further our percapita level of emission is much less compared to the developed countries.[33] This does not mean that India is immune from the climate change threat. The Intergovernmental Panel on Climate Change (IPCC)[34] predicts that glacial melts in the Himalayan region alone will increase flooding, trigger avalanches and landslides, and cause extinction of species and ecosystems.[35] In fact many of the Himalayan Glaciers including the Gangotri, have receded by many meters threatening the natural ecosystem and hydrological cycle causing extreme drought and flood situations.[36] With regard to India marked increase in seasonal surface air temperature is projected into the 21st century, becoming conspicuous after the 2040s.[37] Concentration of droughts is projected in Gujarat and Rajasthan, which are already drought-prone, and in Orissa, which is currently flood-prone.[38] It is estimated that if a one-meter sea level rise were to take place today, it would displace 7 million persons in India.[39] Studies have pointed to a possible loss of 4 to 5 million tonnes in the overall wheat production with every 1 degree centigrade increase in temperature throughout the growing period of the crop.[40] Further it may result in short crop duration periods to the detriment of agricultural yields,[41] As already pointed out the negative impact of climate change will more vigorously affect women, with India being no exception.

Further disastrous events that may be ragged by climate change will not only have severe natural, environmental , economic and social repercussions on women , but will have serious implication with regard to the various Human Rights, fundamental rights and other constitutional rights guaranteed under our constitution. There are various rights that will be affected by climate change. Notable among them are right to life under Art 21 and the expanded and integral rights which is part of Art 21[42] including rights to livelihood, health,[43] clean environment, water, and basic necessities.[44] Further impacts of climate change may affect various directive principles guaranteed under part 1V of the constitution like Art 48 and 48A dealing with agriculture and Environment. It is to be noted that this aspect of climate change has received much less attention from experts and policy makers. But in recent times this knowledge is proving to be ever more valuable in developing countries and should be taken into account in the adaptation of vulnerable communities to Climate Change.

Legislative Response

Addressing the consequences of global warming through climate change management is not a regulatory field that originally belonged to international law - there have been various attempts to tackle its symptoms on the domestic level. [45] Realizing the transboundary effect of climate change and its effect on humanity, In 1988 the World Meteorological Organization ("WMO") and the United Nations Environment Programme ("UNEP") jointly established the IPCC to assess available information on the science, impacts, and economics of climate change and to formulate adaptation and mitigation options.[46] The IPCC has produced a series of reports and technical papers that are standard works of reference for policymakers, scientists and other experts.[47] Various reports of IPCC removed any doubt if any regarding the all pervasiveness of climate change.

In 1990 the IPCC published its influential First Assessment Report on the condition of the global climate system, which served as a starting point for comprehensive UN

General Assembly negotiations.[48] By way of Resolution 45/212 the General Assembly set up the Intergovernmental Negotiating Committee for a Framework Convention on Climate Change, which completed its task of drawing up the Convention by May 1992.[49]

The U.N. Framework Convention on Climate Change: Beginning of International Attention

The UNFCCC was adopted in 1992 with the objective to stabilize GHG concentrations in the atmosphere at an environmentally safe level.[50] It mandates the member states to promote and cooperate in the development and diffusion of technologies to reduce GHG emissions.[51] Because the member states recognized that countries differ in their capacities to achieve the goals of the convention, they established several means, including financing and technology transfer, by which countries could cooperate to meet these goals.[52] It should be noted that the convention did not set any binding GHG emission targets.[53] It forms a framework for further action and cooperation on the issue of climate change. A key aspect of the treaty is its division of nations into "Annex I" (forty-one industrialized countries and economies in transition, such as the former Soviet Union and Eastern European states) and "Annex II" (twenty- four wealthy members of the Organization of Economic Cooperation and Development).[54] The remaining countries of the world are described as "non-Annex I" countries. This division became the guiding force even in Kyoto protocol. Convention draws on various principles like Precautionary rule, relates to intergenerational equity, Public trust , Polluters principle etc. The concept of common but differentiated responsibility runs through the width and breadth of the convention.[55] This formed the basis of UFCCC requirement for the developing countries to develop in a sustainable manner and address the adverse effects of climate change through adaptation. This responsibility is unique to developing countries in the sense that it requires developing countries to take on board sustainable development, framed in the climate context as sensitivity to GHG emissions use,[56] The UNFCCC requires developed countries to address climate change through specific mitigation commitments.The convention has also established an Annual Conference of Parties (COP) to oversee its implementation in the member countries.

One year later the Conference of the Parties (COP), held its first meeting (COP 1). It found out that the commitments under the Convention were insufficient to meet the challenges posed by climate change. Negotiations were commenced to supplement the Convention in accordance with a protocol under Article 17 [57] layiing down further commitments for meeting UNFCCC goals. As a result, the Kyoto Protocol (KP) was adopted in 1997 by COP 3.[58]

The Kyoto Protocol: Beginning of Responsibility

The Kyoto Protocol is a product of the Berlin Mandate Process. Adopted by the first COP, the Berlin Mandate proposed strengthening the commitments of Annex I Parties through the adoption of a Protocol or another legal instrument. [59]

The Kyoto Protocol is an international law instrument setting stringent, legally binding emission reduction targets for six GHGs across a five-year commitment period.[60] Adopted in Kyoto, Japan in 1997, it was the first protocol to the UNFCCC.[61] So far, 182 member parties have ratified the Kyoto Protocol.[62] The GHGs regulated by the Kyoto Protocol include CO_2, methane (CH_4), nitrous oxide (N_2O), sulfur dioxide (SO_2), sulfur hexafluoride (SF_6), hydrofluorocarbons ("HFCs"), and perfluorocarbons ("PFCs"). [63]The protocol commits developed countries to specific emission reduction targets, but there is no binding obligation for developing countries to reduce emissions or cap the growth of emissions.[64] The group target for the thirty-seven industrial countries and the European Community is a reduction in emissions to an average of five percent against the

1990 level over the period 2008 - 2012.[65] According to the protocol, target emission reductions can be achieved through national clean energy initiatives and through market-oriented, flexible mechanisms such as emissions trading and the Clean Development Mechanism ("CDM"). Four flexibility mechanisms under the KyotoProtocol that can be utilized by these industrialized countries: "Bubble" Mechanism (Article 4),[66] Emissions Trading (Article 17),[67] Joint Implementation (Article 6),[68] and Clean Development Mechanism (Article 12). Bubble Mechanism refers to the European Union member countries that agreed to have a collective QELRO of 8 percent, regardless of the actual individual countries' reductions. Emissions Trading (ET) refers to exchanging assigned amount of emissions between Annex I countries, expectedly between rich Annex I countries. Joint Implementation (JI) involves investment by an Annex I country in another Annex I country, with emissions reductions that are credited to the investing country. Clean Development Mechanism (CDM), is a mechanism similar to JI, except that it applies only for investment in developing countries, or countries not included in Annex I of FCCC.[69]

The Kyoto Protocol is an historic milestone. It is the first, and only, binding international agreement that sets targets to reduce the greenhouse gas emissions that cause climate change .The adoption of the Protocol strengthened institutional and legal frames of the climate change regime but, at the same time, it created new challenges to the parties, such as the need for a detailed composition of flexibility mechanisms and the question of equity between developed and developing countries.

Bali Action Plan

In 2005, at COP-11, states agreed to start a series of "dialogues" to consider long-term cooperation under the UNFCCC "without prejudice to any future negotiations, commitments process, framework or mandate under the Convention."[70] At Bali in 2008, at COP-13, negotiations began for the post-Kyoto regime 2012 and beyond, the Parties to the UNFCCC established the Ad Hoc Working Group on Long-term Cooperative Action (AWGLCA) as a subsidiary body under the UNFCCC. The Bali Action Plan sets out a roadmap that includes four building blocks: mitigation, adaptation, technology transfer, and financial resources. [71] In Bali it was agreed that the post-2012 arrangement concerning climate change is to be agreed at COP15 and COP/MOP5, which is to be held in Copenhagen in December 2009.

Analysis of international climate change regime reveals that the UN Framework Convention on Climate Change (UNFCCC), failed to recognize the gender aspects of climate change and omits the issues of gender equality and women's participation entirely. Also, its Kyoto Protocol, that outlines reductions in greenhouse gasses until 2012, fails in integrating a gender perspective in its operationalization and mechanisms, such as the Clean Development Mechanism.

In recent times some efforts have been initiated to bring gender concern to the forefront of climate Change agenda. The General Debate of the UN General Assembly and the High-Level Event on Climate Change, September 2007, shows that climate change has risen to the very top of the international policy agenda.[72] On that occasion a 'Roundtable on Gender and Climate Change' was convened by WEDO and the Council of Women World Leaders. Consequently, the International Women Leaders Global Security Summit in New York, November 2007, acknowledged that climate change poses significant security risks, particularly for women, and that women have to be included in decision-making at all levels.[73]

The only initiative which is considerate and representative of women's participation occurred in Bali .For the first time in UNFCCC history, a worldwide network of women,– women for climate justice, was established. The group published several position papers articulating the women's and gender perspectives on the most pressing issues under negotiation. And for the first time a range of activities on women's and gender issues was organized by various organisations and institutions. And they met with interest, increasing awareness, and increased expression of commitment to gender justice from a number of stakeholders.[74] Bali declaration also saw the Global Gender and Climate Change Alliance of UN organizations; IUCN and WEDO along with other international organizations were established.[75]

NGOs, and International Organizations like IUCN have started expressing their strong commitment to gender mainstreaming in climate change policies. Thus, it appears that half of world s population is finally beginning to be heard and accepted as one of the fundamental and indispensable principles of mitigating climate change and adapting to its impacts. Feminist movement has played a considerable role in slowly bringing about a gender perspective attitude in climate change discourse. They pointed out that the present climate change regime mainly focuses on technologies and economic instruments which need to be widened. They questioned the patriarchal oriented policy systems and emphasized the need to convert the climate policy to put care and justice in its prime agenda. The lack of gender perspectives in the current climate process not only violates women's human rights, but it also leads to shortcomings in the efficiency and effectiveness of climate related measures and instruments. It seems that these patiently continued activities, including through tough times, are finally paying off.

Gender Concerns and International Sustainable Development

An analysis of various international instruments suggest that climate regime can definitely take the assistance of other instruments which as incorporated gender concerns as part of their focus. Agenda 21, the final outcome of Rio De Janeiro offers a roadmap towards sustainable development taking into account gender concerns.[76] Chapter 24, entitled "Global Action for Women towards Sustainable Development", calls upon governments to eliminate all obstacles to women's full involvement in sustainable development and public life. Agenda 21 is to be achieved through policies and plans aiming at promoting equity in all spheres of society, including women's key involvement in decision making and environmental management.[77]

Further World Summit on Sustainable Development in Johannesburg, stressed on the importance of women's equal access and full participation in decision-making for sustainable development.[78] The Johannesburg Plan of Action emphasized on mainstreaming gender perspectives in the overall policies and strategies of sustainable developemt,[79] It aimed at elimination of all kinds of discrimination against women and stressed on the improvement of the status, health and economic welfare of women and girls through full and equal access to land, economic opportunities, credit, education and health-care service. The Convention to Combat Desertification 1994 (UNCCD, 1994) closely follows the Johannesburg Declaration and clearly recognizes the role of women in rural livelihoods and encourages the full participation of women and men in the implementation of the convention.[80] The UNCCD stresses the important role played by women in regions affected by desertification and/or drought, particularly in rural areas in developing countries. It instructs national action programs to provide effective participation of women and men, particularly resources users, including farmers and pastoralists and their organizations.

Although the 1992 Convention on Biodiversity recognizes the role of women in conservation and sustainable use of biological diversity and affirms the need for the full participation of women at all levels of policy making and implementation, only recently have steps been taken to ensure gender mainstreaming in the convention's implementation.[81]

The clearest mandate on gender and disasters, which is easily extended to climate-induced disasters, is the Hyogo Framework for Action that emerged from the World Conference on Disaster Reduction (2005).[82] The Hyogo Framework states that "a gender perspective should be integrated into all disaster risk management policies, plans and decision-making processes, including those related to risk assessment, early warning, information management, and education and training."[83]

Further any discussion on womens rights will not be complete without mention of The Millennium Declaration 2000.[84] Declaration calls on signatories to promote equality between sexes and the empowerment of women as effective means to combat poverty, hunger and diseases, and promote a truly sustainable development. The emerging Millennium Development Goals are of particular interest to gender equality in climate change discourse through their parallel goals of women's empowerment and environmental sustainability. [85]Although in practice, these goals are often still operationalized separately, together these establish a platform of fundamental interrelated values on gender and climate change which today revolves around the key areas of : mitigation, adaptation, technology and finance.

National Action Plan on Climate Change and Gender

India's first direct policy response in terms of climate cange was unveiled in te form of a National Action Plan on Climate Change(NAPCC) in 2008The NAPCC has laid down a national strategy on climate change with regard to adaptation and mitigation of greenhouse gas emissions, and is the first explicit response to climate change.[86] The action plan briefly recognizes the special vulnerability of women with regard to climate change. It states "The impacts of climate change could prove particularly severe for women. With climate change, there would be increasing scarcity of water, reduc-tion in yields of forest biomass, and increased risks to human health with children, women and the elderly in a household becoming the most vulnerable. With the possibility of decline in availability of foodgrains, the threat of malnutrition may also increase. All these would add to deprivations that women already encounter and so in each of the Adaptation pro-grammes, special attention should be paid to the aspects of gender."[87] Further with regard to energy conservation and use Te plan points that "While several households, especially in the rural areas, continue to use biomass for cooking in traditional cookstoves, which leads to high levels of indoor air pollution and poses a major health risk especially to women and children."[88]

Though the action plan has tried to address the issue of gender and stressed on the need to address their welfare. The impact of the Plan on them is questionable. On the contrary, the implementation of the Plan could impact them adversely if the economic burden of the adaptation strategies is not supported by the government. The majority of the women who is vulnerable to climate change is poorly equipped to cope effectively with the adversities of climate change due to low capabilities, weak institutional mechanisms, and lack of access to adequate resources. The plan does not envisage any special strategies or measures to alter or a change these.

Adaptation

Present climate change regime revolves around the key areas of : mitigation, adaptation, technology and finance. The elementary goal of adaptation strategies is the decrease in the vulnerabilities of climate induced change in order to protect and enhance the livelihoods of poor people. Experience and studies shows that adaptation to climate change or indeed climate variability is dependent on issues such as wealth, technological power, access to information, all of which are major problem areas for women. However, women can be key agents of adaptation to climate change. Women's specific knowledge of maintaining biodiversity, through the conservation and domestication of wild edible plant seeds and food crop breeding, is key to adapting to climate change more effectively. Their responsibilities in households, communities position them well to develop strategies for adapting to changing environmental realties.[89] They develop a broad knowledge and experiences regarding their environment[90] which are being evaluated constantly and changed when the environmental and social conditions of their surroundings.

Mitigation

Women can play a positive role in climate change mitigation Generally they are engaged in a number of traditional activities such as brick making, charcoal making solid waste management and agro-processing. In all these activities energy efficiency can lead to CO2 mitigation and their role in mitigation in these areas can be vital. [91] Women in urban areas can implement energy efficiency programmes at the household level through lighting, and use of appliances etc, while women in rural areas may be encouraged to use biomass and biogas for fuel generation, and switch to solar energy. The development of Clean Development Mechanisms (CDM), through carbon sequestration from afforestation and reforestation can also be done by poor rural women .[92]

Constructing a Post 2012 Gender Sensitive Climate Change Regime

Already hectic efforts are being made to construct and evolve a post 2012 climate regime which will satisfy the concerns of both the developed and developing countries. It is imperative that designing any equitable climate regime can not ignore the voice of half of its population. It should be noted that women are not just helpless victims of climate change – they are powerful agents of change and their participation and contribution is crucial and critical for the success of any climate policy. Women can assist or deter in climate change mitigation and adaptation issues such as energy consumption, deforestation, burning of vegeta-tion, population growth and economic growth, development of scientific research and technologies, policy making, among many others.

Efforts aimed at creating greater awareness and understanding of the complex links between gender equality and climate change can help to build the capacity of the poor, especially poor women, to adapt to the impacts of, and take action on, climate change which will make the climate regime more sensitive and justice oriented.

Policy and Programming Considerations should Include

- Government should analyze and identify gender specific impacts and protection measures related to floods, droughts, diseases, and other environmental changes and disasters.
- Government should develop strategies to enhance women's access to and control over natural resources, in order to reduce poverty, protect environmental resources, and ensure that women and poor communities can better cope with climate change. Measures that provide present and future benefits are required to increase the re-silience of people's livelihoods, diminish gender inequality, increase awareness of climate change effects and prepare them for future changes.[93]
- Women, like men, should have equitable access to the benefits of market-based approaches to curbing climate change (e.g., the Clean Development Mechanism). CDM should fund projects that make renewable energy technologies more acces-sible to women and that can fulfil their household needs.[94]
- The UNFCCC should develop a gender strategy, promote women representatives as official focal points, invest in

gender-specific climate change research, and establish a system for the use of gender-sensitive indicators and criteria for governments to use in national reporting to the UNFCCC Secretariat, adaptation planning, or projects under the Clean Development Mechanism (CDM).

- The international climate change negotiation process – as well as climate policies at regional, national and local levels – must adopt the principles of gender equity and equality at all stages: in research, in analysis, and in the design and implementation of making use of technologies that are accessible, beneficial, and acceptable to both male and female stakeholders; [95] Involve local women in Climate Change risk assessment and monitoring.
- Given that women's knowledge and participation has been critical to the survival of entire communities in disaster situations, government should take cognizance of women's specialized skills in different aspects of their livelihood and natural resource management strategies and utilize those that lend themselves to mitigation and adaptation.
- Women's participation in climate change related debates and United Nations[96]
- Take women's physical, psychological, social and economic vulnerabilities into account in community-based disaster preparedness and response plans.
- Enhance gender equality policies, legislation and strategies.
- Promoting environmental friendly -burning fuel for household use, which will help to reduce air pollution and harmful emissions, and will benefit women by cutting their annual cooking costs by 25 percent;

Conclusion

Climate Change is not only a major environmental, economic and scientific concern but also a significant social and gender concern that constrain the sustainability and the resilience of societies. Climate change and the adverse environmental events clearly have a bearing on development and have profound implications for society and its existence including women.

As a product of their social roles, women perform a fundamental role in their communities in reducing the risk of climate change and searching for strategies of adaptation. Faced with the manifestations of Climate Change, their knowledge and experience should be taken into account when planning adaptation processes for vulnerable communities. However, it is important to consider that in these processes men also intervene and could play decisive roles. Therefore, it is necessary to promote strategies for adaptation through inclusive and consultative processes that give participation to both men and women exposed to risks, taking into account the needs and expectations of both, and addressing a perspective of gender equity. In this sense, adaptation processes will act as an opportunity for questioning and changing traditional gender relations in society. Mostly men have modified the planet's environment throughout history. The challenging issue for our lifetime is the increase in the scale of this modification and whether or not these changes in climate can be accommodated and reversed using the women's special existing capacity to act or adapt.

References

1 Sebastian Oberthur& Hermann E. O, "The Kyoto Protocol" International Polity, 27 (2000).

2 Vincent, K.: "Uncertainty in Adaptive apacity and the Importance of Scale," Global Environ. Change, 17, 12–24, (2007).

3 IPCC, Summary for Policymakers, in Climate Change 2007: The

Physical Science Basis Contribution of Working Group to the Fourth Assessment Report of the Intergovernmental Panel on Climate Change (S. Solomon, D. Qin, M. Manning, Z. Chen, M. Marquis, K.B. Averyt, M. Tignor, & H.L. Miller eds., Cambridge University Press, Cambridge, United Kingdom.

4 Id.

5 Stern Review on The Economics of Climate Change Stern Report, part 11 Impact of Climate change,(2007).

6 Jason Morrison,"Water Sarcity and Climate Change: Growing risks for Busineses and Investors, Ceres report (2009).

7 IPCC, Summary for Policymakers, in Climate Change 2001, Impacts, Adaptation, and Vulnerability. Report of Working Group II of the IPCC.

8 Drexhage, J. "The World Conservation Union (IUCN) Climate Change Situation. Analysis". Final Report. IISD-IUCN. Switzerland, (2006).

9 Id.

10 Climate Change: Impacts, Vulnerabilities and Adaptation in Developing Countries,UNFCC available on http://unfccc.int/files/essential_background/background_publications_htmlpdf/application/txt/pub_07_impacts.pdf (Last accessed on 3-05-2009).

11 "Gender Equality and Climate Change ,Why Consider Gender Equality When Taking Action on Climate Change?", Canadian International Development Agency, (2002).

12 Eliamep, "Gender, Climate Change and Human Security Lessons from Bangladesh, Ghana and Senegal, "Women's Environment and Development Organization, May (2008).

13 The convention recognized for the first time in international law that the conservation of biological diversity is "a common concern of humankind" and is an integral part of the development process. The agreement covers all ecosystems, species, and genetic resources. It links traditional conservation efforts to the economic goal of using biological resources sustainable. Convention was in Rio de Janeiro in June 1992.

14 Stige, L.C. Thousand-year-long Chinese time series reveals climatic forcing of decadal locust dynamics." Proceedings of the National Academy of Sciences 104(41): 16188–16193,(2007).

15 Supra note 11.

16 Id.

17 "Women: The Key to Food Security". International Food Policy Research Institute. June 2000available on <http://www.ifpri.org/pubs/ib/ib3.pdf>.Last (Accessed on 10-03-2009).

18 Junaid Razak,"Emergency Medical care in Developing Countries Is it worth while,"Bull world Healt Organ, Vol 80, No 11 Genebra, (2002).

19 Patt, Anthony, Angie Dazé and Pablo Suarez, 2007. Gender and Climate Change Vulnerability: What's the Problem, What's the Solution? Paper presented at the International Women Leaders,,Global Security Summit,New York 15-17 November (2007).

20 Aguilar, L. Fact Sheet on: Fisheries and aquaculture in coastal zones. Costa Rica. IUCN.(2004).

21 Donner, S.D. Model-Based Assessment of the Role of Human-Induced Climate Change in the 2005 Carib-Bean Coral Bleaching Event. Proceedings of the National Academy of Sciences 104(13),(2007).

22 Loreana Aguiler "Gender and Climate Change", available on http://generoyambiente.org/admin/admin_biblioteca/documentos/Factsheet%20ClimateChange.pdflast visited on 3-02-1009).

23 Aguilar, L. Fact Sheet on: Climate Change and Disaster Mitigation. Costa Rica. IUCN, (2004).

24 Y. Carvajal-Escobar 1, M. Quintero-Angel 1, and M. Garc´ýa-Vargas 2 Women's role in adapting to climate change and variability, Adv. Geosci., 14, 277–280, (2008).

25 Id.

26 Enarson. E.: Gender Issues in Natural Disasters, Talking Points and Research Needs, in: Focus Programme on Crisis Response and Reconstruction Workshop, 48, ILO, Geneva, 30 p., (2000).

27 Id.

28 Lambrou, Y. and Piana, G.: Gender: the Missing Component in the Response to Climate Change, Food and Agriculture Organization of the United Nations, Rome, available at: http://www.fao.org/ sd/dim pe1/docs/pe1 051001d1b.pdf, 46 pp., (2005)Last visited on 3-06-2009.

29 Id.

30 "Climate Change Impacts On The United States, The Potential Consequences of Climate Variability and Change," National Assessment Synthesis Team, US Global Change Research Program.

31 Supra note 22 See, Loreana.

32 Development Data Group of the Development Economics Vice Presidency and the Environment Department of the World Bank, The Little Green Data Book (International Bank for Reconstruction and Development, 2007) (2001), available at http://siteresources.worldbank.org/INTDATASTA/64199955- 1178226923002/21322619/LGDB2007.pdf.<Last visited on 12-04-2009).

33 Navigating the Numbers : Green House Data and Iinternatioal Climate Policy— Part, Cha 4 percapita Emissions, 2001.

34 The Intergovernmental Panel on Climate Change, comprising scientific experts from a select number of countries, was established in 1988 by the Executive Council of the World Meteorological Organization (WMO), with support from UNEP, to identify "uncertainties and gaps in "present knowledge" about climate change and its potential impacts; gather information "to evaluate policy implications" and "response strategies;" "review... national/international policies" regarding GHGs; and carry out "scientific and environmental assessments regarding GHG emissions and transfer them for relevant governmental and intergovernmental agencies.

35 Climate Change 2007 ,Impacts, Adaptability and Vulnerability, IPCC, Working Group II Contribution to the Intergovernmental Panel on Climate Change Fourth Assessment Report, Summary for Policy Makers (2007), available at http://www.ipcc.ch/pdf/assessment-report/ar4/wg2/ar4-wg2-spm.pdf Last visited on4-06-2009).

36 Emily Wax, "A Sacred River Endangered by Global Warming", Wash. Post, June 17, (2007), at A14, available at http://www.washingtonpost.com/wp-dyn/content/article/2007/06/16/AR2007061600461.html.Last visited on 3-05-2009.

37 India's Initial National Communications to the United Nations Framework Convention on Climate Change, Ministry of Environment and Forests, New Delhi, (2004).

38 Climate Change and India: Impacts, Policy Responses and a Framework for EU-India Cooperation, DG Internal Policies of the Union Policy Department Economic and Scientific Policy.

39 Jyoti K. Parikh and Kirit Parikh, Climate Change: India's Perceptions, Positions, Policies And Possibilities, Climate Change and Development, OECD Discussion paper, (2002).

40 Surinder Sud, "Agriculture may Decline due to Climate Change", Business Standard, New Delhi January 21, (2008).

41 Jayant Sathaye, P.R. Shukla, & N.H. Ravindranath," Climate Change, Sustainable Development and India: Global and National Concerns, 90 No. 3 Current Science,314, 314-25 (2006).

42 Article 21 states, "[n]o person shall be deprived of his life or personal liberty except according to procedure established by law." India Const. Art. 21.

43 Bandhua Mukti Morcha v. India, A.I.R. 1984 S.C. 802.

44 Olga Tellis v. Bombay Municipal Corporation, A.I.R. 1985 S.C. 180.

45 Examples include the Clean Air Act (1990) of the US and its amendments, as well as the South Coast Regional Clean Air Incentives Market (RECLAIM), also foreseeing pollution trading. See Micheal S. Smith, Murky Precedent Meets Hazy Air: The Compact Clause and the Regional Greenhouse Gas Initiative, 34 Boston College Environmental Affairs Law Review 387-416 (2007).

46 Intergovernmental Panel On Climate Change, Summary for Policymakers, in IPCC Special Report: Methodological And Technological ssues In Technology Transfer 3 (2000).

47 IPCC REPORT, The IPCC provides Assessment Reports at regular intervals on the state of knowledge on climate change. Supplementary to the Assessment Reports and often at the request of other environmental conventions, such as the UNFCCC, the IPCC prepares Special Reports and Technical Papers, which focus on a particular topic (e.g. technology transfer).

48 Supra note 7.

49 Daniel Bodansky, The United Nations Framework Convention on Climate Change: A Commentary, 18 Yale Journal Of International Law 461-474 (1993).

50 United Nations Framework Convention on Climate Change, May 9, 1992, S. TREATY DOC. NO. 102-38, 1771 U.N.T.S. 107 [hereinafter UNFCCC TREATY] (entered into force Mar. 21, 1994), archived at http:// www.webcitation.org/5at2iBAl5.(Last visited on 5-04-2009 s as "those gaseous constituents of the atmosphere, both natural and anthropogenic, that absorb and re-emit infrared radiation".

51 Id Preamble.

52 Id Art 4.1(c), 4.3, 4.5.

53 UNFCCC, Fact Sheet: The Kyoto Protocol.

54 Supra note 35 UNFCCC Info Kit, at Information Sheet 18.

55 The principle of Common but Differentiated Responsibility (CBDR) is one of the cornerstones of sustainable development. It has emerged as a principle of International Environmental Law and has been explicitly formulated in the context of the 1992 Rio Earth Summit. It finds its origins in equity considerations and equity principles in international law. It informs in particular the United Nations Framework Convention on Climate Change (UNFCCC) and the Kyoto protocol. The Rio Declaration Principle 7 view of the different contributions to global environmental degradation, States have common but differentiated responsibilities. The developed countries acknowledge the responsibility that they bear in the international pursuit of sustainable development in view of the pressures their societies place

on the global environment and of the technologies and financial resources they command." Similar language exists in the Framework Convention on Climate Change; parties should act to protect the climate system "on the basis of equality and in accordance with their common but differentiated responsibilities and respective capabilities".

56 Article 4(1) (f), FCCC (requiring all countries to take climate change considerations into account, to the extent feasible, in their relevant social, economic and environmental policies).

57 Art. 17 UNFCCC allows for the adoption of protocols by the Conference of the Parties by consensus; the Conference of the Parties is open only to the Parties of the Convention.

58 By decision 1/CP.3. So far the Kyoto Protocol has received 170 ratifications (18 April 2007). For the reasons behind the resistance of one of the most substantial GHG emitter, the United States, see Cass R. Sunstein, Of Montreal and Kyoto: A Tale of Two Protocols, 31 HARVARD ENVIRONMENTAL LAW REVIEW 1-65 (2007).

59 Decision 1/CP.1, The Berlin Mandate: Review of Adequacy of Articles 4, paragraph 2, subparagraph (a) and (b), of the Convention, including proposals related to a Protocol and decisions on follow-up, contained in Report of the Conference of Parties on its first session held at Berlin from 28 March to 7 April 1995, FCCC/CP/1995/7/Add.1 (1995).

60 David Freestone, The UN Framework Convention on Climate Change, the Kyoto Protocol, and the Kyoto Mechanisms, in Legal Aspects Of Implementation The Kyoto Protocol Mechanisms: Making Kyoto Work, 3 (David Freestone & Charlotte Streck eds., Oxford University Press (2005).

61 Kyoto Protocol to the United Nations Framework Convention on Climate Change, Dec. 10, 1997, U.N. Doc. FCCC/CP/1997/L.7/Add.1, 37 I.L.M. 22 available at http://www.webcitation.org/5at2y1ixN (following ratification by Russia, the Kyoto Protocol entered into force on 16 February 2005).Last visited on 5-05-2009.

62 UNFCCC, Kyoto Protocol Status of Ratification, archived at http://www.webcitation.org/5at33npAB. Last visited on 13-05-2009 184 countries and one regional economic integration organization (the EEC) have deposited instruments of ratification, accession, approval or acceptance. Id.

63 Kyoto Protocol, supra note 61, Annex A.

64 Kyoto Protocol, supra note 61, Art. 3 and Annex B.

65 Kyoto Facts, supra note 53, at 1.

66 Id Article 4 Any Parties included in Annex I that have reached an

agreement to fulfil their commitments under Article 3 jointly, shall be deemed to have met those commitments provided that their total combined aggregate anthropogenic carbon dioxide equivalent emissions of the greenhouse gases listed in Annex A do not exceed their assigned amounts calculated pursuant to their quantified emission limitation and reduction commitments inscribed in Annex B and in accordance with the provisions of Article 3. The respective emission level allocated to each of the Parties to the agreement shall be set out in that agreement.

67 Id Article 17 The Conference of the Parties shall define the relevant principles, modalities, rules and guidelines, in particular for verification, reporting and accountability for emissions trading. The Parties included in Annex B may participate in emissions trading for the purposes of fulfilling their commitments under Article 3. Any such trading shall be supplemental to domestic actions for the purpose of meeting quantified emission limitation and reduction commitments under that Article.

68 Id Article 6 For the purpose of meeting its commitments under Article 3, any Party included in Annex I may transfer to, or acquire from, any other such Party emission reduction units resulting from projects aimed at reducing anthropogenic emissions by sources or enhancing anthropogenic removals by sinks of greenhouse gases in any sector of the economy, provided that:a) Any such project has the approval of the Parties involved; (b) Any such project provides a reduction in emissions by sources, or an enhancement of removals by sinks, that is additional to any that would otherwise.

69 http://cd4cdm.org/Publications/CDM&SustainDevelop_literature.pdf (last visited on 19-02-2009).

70 United Nations Framework Convention on Climate Change, Bali Action Plan, Decision -/CP.13, at 1 (Dec. 15, 2007), available at http:/ / unfccc.int/files/meetings/cop_13/application/pdf/cp_bali_action.pdf (last visited 3-04- 2009).

71 Id.

72 UN Secretary-General convenes world leaders to build momentum for climate change talks in Bali available on http://www.un.org/ climatechange/2007highlevel/Last visited on 6-05-2009).

73 The International Women Leaders Global Security Summit provides women leaders a forum to discuss, evaluate and endorse meaningful strategies for global security. Participants include current and former heads of state and government, influential ministers and leaders of inter-governmental and nongovernmental organizations who are committed to addressing critical security issues.

74 Ulrike Röhr, Minu Hemmati, A Gender-Sensitive Climate Regime? Available on http://www.gendercc.net/fileadmin/inhalte/Dokumente/UNFCCC_conferences/Conclusions_COP13.pdf(last visited on4-04-2009).

75 Supra note 12 see Eliamp.

76 Agenda 21 is a programme run by the United Nations (UN) related to sustainable development. It is a comprehensive blueprint of action to be taken globally, nationally and locally by organizations of the UN, governments, and major groups in every area in which humans impact on the environment.

77 Id, Chapter 24.

78 Johannesburg Summit 2002 – the World Summit on Sustainable Development – brought together tens of thousands of participants, including heads of State and Government, national delegates and leaders from non-governmental organizations (NGOs), businesses and other major groups to focus the world's attention and direct action toward meeting difficult challenges, including improving people's lives and conserving our natural resources in a world that is growing in population, with ever-increasing demands for food, water, shelter, sanitation, energy, health services and economic security.

79 Report of the World Summit on Sustainable Development, states "We are committed to ensuring that women.s empowerment, emancipation and gender equality are integrated in all the activities encompassed within Agenda 21, the Millennium development goals6 and the Plan of Implementation of the Summit".

80 The United Nations Convention to Combat Desertification in Those Countries Experiencing Serious Drought and/or Desertification, Particularly in Africa is a Convention to combat desertification and mitigate the effects of drought through national action programs that incorporate long-term strategies supported by international cooperation and partnership arrangements.

81 Supra note 12.

82 The Hyogo Framework for Action 2005 – 2015: Building the Resilience of Nations and Communities to Disasters, was adopted by 168 Governments at the World Conference on Disaster Reduction held in Kobe, Japan in January 2005.

83 Id.

84 United Nations Millennium Declaration, Ares//55/L.2).

85 Id.

86 National Action Plan on Climate Change.

87 Id.

88 Id.

89 Women's Environment and Development organization,2007. WEDO was established in 1990 Since its inception, WEDO has been a leader in organizing women for international conferences and actions. In 1992, WEDO organized the World Women's Congress for a Healthy Planet, bringing together more than 1,500 women from 83 countries to work jointly on a strategy for the UN Conference on Environment and Development (UNCED). The result was Women's Action Agenda 21, an outline for a healthy and peaceful planet that was the basis for introducing gender equality in the official UNCED final documents Agenda 21 and the Rio Declaration.

90 Ariyabandu, M.: Women, The Risk Managers in Natural Disasters, in: Gender Equality & Disasters Risk Reduction Workshop, 2004available at: http://www.ssri.hawaii.edu/research/GDWwebsite/pdf/ Last accessed on 6-04-2009.

91 Lambrou, Y. and Piana, G.: Gender: The Missing Component in the Response to Climate Change, Food and Agriculture Organization of the United Nations, Rome, available at: http://www.fao.org/ sd/dim pe1/ docs/pe1 051001d1b.pdf, 46 pp., 2005 Last accesse don 4-04-2009.

92 Dr. Jyoti Parikh, "Mainstreaming Gender into Climate Change Policies", Integrated Research and Action for Development (IRADe), New Delhi commissioned by UNDP, India.

93 Supra note 22 See, Loreana.

94 Liane Schalatek, "Gender and Climate Finance: Double Mainstreaming for sustainable Development," Heinrich Böll Foundation North America, May 2009.

95 Supra note 11 See Gender.

96 Supra note 92 see Jyoti.

7

Information and Communication Technology and Pornography: A Threat to the Dignity of Women

Introduction

The Department of Telecommunications has directed all Indian Internet Service Providers (ISPs) to block access to the popular Indian adult toon website, Savitabhabhi.com. The site rates as the 82nd most popular Indian website. Controller of Certifying Authorities (CCA) said they were forced to take such action after receiving several complaints. Since its launch in March 2008, Savitabhabhi.com has acquired a cult following with its unique plot that narrates the exploits of its beguiling central figure, Savita Bhabhi.[1] The site's popularity did not come without its perils. The portrayal of a married Indian woman as wildly promiscuous raised the hackles of many in a largely conservative nation. One of them, Bangalore-based N. Vijayashankar, waged a sustained campaign against Savitabhabhi, complaining to the government's Computer Emergency Response Team (CERT-IN) as well as the Director General of Police in Karnataka. He concluded "Cartoons are a more participative medium.[2] In fact the cartoon has reportedly influenced an 11-year-old boy, in Bangalore, who sent out an obscene mail to one of his teachers. The teacher complained to the cops and the Bangalore Police booked the child under the ITA 2000 law which carries a possible jail term of five years.[3]

The problem did not subside with the ban, a support site, Savesavita.com, has already been set up to protest the ban on the site. One blogger wrote "I think Savitabhabhi.com should not be banned by the government as there are already so many porn sites running on the internet. Ban of Savitabhabhi.com is not good for the development of India. If any body want to see the porn sites then he can view those sites on the internet on one click. So I think it is not fruitful for India to ban on Savitabhabhi.com. The Chapter analyses the impact of new Information and Communication Technology (ICT) revolution on Pornography. Chapter discusses the impact of pornography on women and critically analyses the international and national legal response in this regard.

Information and Communication Technology Revolution: Challenges and opportunities for Women

A century and more after the industrial revolution, we are in the throes of another major shift in human civilization – the information and communication technology (ICT) revolution that has given birth to the "information society" It has been recognized as a potent force that can transform the development pace and status of a country.

The potential benefits for women from the use of ICT are enormous. For women as a whole, ICTs offer immense possibilities for reducing poverty by providing income generating opportunities, overcoming women's isolation, giving women a voice, improving governance and advancing gender equality. Despite economic and socio-cultural barriers to women's use of Information and Communication Technology

(ICT), when women are able to use them productively, they can substantially improve their lives and increase their income. In fact they have already proved their useful in: health care delivery; distance education; enhancing rural productivity through access to market information and access to finance; promoting empowerment and participation in national and international policy processes; improving service delivery by governments; improving environmental monitoring and response systems; and facilitating environmental activism.[4]

Relation between women and ICT is not as simple as the above sited benefits suggests. Many consider technology as gender neutral. Others treat it as a weapon of female exploitation **(Table 1).**

Table :1 Women's Relationship with Technology

Approach	*Primary Thrust*	*Central concepts*	*Critique/Comment*
Liberal Approach	To uncover the women hidden from history	Sees technology as inherently neutral. Sees the challenge to be improving women's access to technology in a society that is gendered by stereo typical sex roles.	Does not critique technology itself
Marxist Approach	To examine the social relations of technology in terms of class	Sees women's exclusion from technology as due to the gender division of labour, and the historical and cultural view of technology as masculine. Sees technology as reflecting male power as well as capitalist domination.	Technology still seenas neutral and "misused" undercapitalism
Eco-feminist Approach	To show thattechnology, like science, is part of	Gives value to "feminine"	Takes an essentialist position, seeinggender

	the masculine project of the domination and control of women and nature.	knowledge and skills arising from women's biology and presumed closeness to nature. Has been used to critique military and reproductive technologies.	as (at leastpartly) biological
Third-world and Subsistence Perspectives	To argue the in appropriateness of estern/modern technologies to the Third World.	Challenges western systems of knowledge and technology by asserting that these are colonising and displace local knowledge and experience. Offers a new vision of technology that is democratic, non-colonial, and nonpatriarchal.	Puts too much emphasison people based knowledge systems, rejecting possible adaptation of modern technologies for progressive purposes.
Gendered / "technology as culture" approach	To reject the view that technology isinherently neutral or inherently masculine	Understands gender and technology as cultural processes which can be negotiated and transformed. The relationship between gender and technology is seen as the core issue. Technology is understood to be 'shaped by local histories, geographical conditions, and every day cultural practices...'	Based on the interactions between social power relations and the culture of technology.

Source : Wood 2000

These approaches have adopted a varied approach to the relation ship between women and technology. Whatever may be the merits and demerits of these approaches practical realities suggest that women have always been excluded from science and also from the creation, design and use of technology. While there is an overall recognition of the potential of ICT as a tool for the promotion of gender equality and the empowerment of women, a "gender divide" and digital divide has also been identified, reflected in the lower numbers of women accessing and using ICT compared with men. Unless this gender divide is specifically addressed, there is a risk that ICT may exacerbate existing inequalities between women and men and create new forms of inequality.[5] In many societies, women's and men's access to and use of technology are rooted in behavioral, cultural, and religious traditions:

- Cultural and social attitudes are often unfavorable to women's participation in the fields of science and technology, which limits their opportunities in the area of ICT.
- Women are often financially dependent on men or do not have control over economic resources, which makes accessing ICT services more difficult.
- Allocation of resources for education and training often favors boys and men.
- In some societies, women's seclusion from the public arena makes access to community telecenters difficult. [6]

In order to maximize the potentials of ICT in effecting gender equality and women's empowerment, there is a need to consciously integrate a gender perspective in ICT and improve our ability in identifying and analysing gender and ICT issues. In addition, the impact of the digital gender divide needs to be contextualized within the reality that women make up the majority of the poor and are part of the deeper end of this divide.[7] New communications and information technologies have created a global revolution in communications, access to information, and media delivery. Along with the various benefits that has been brought along with the new ICT, these new communications and information technologies are facilitating the sexual exploitation of women and girls locally, nationally and transnational mainly through pornography. The sexual exploitation of women and children through pornography is a global human rights crisis that is being escalated by the use of new technologies.

Pornography

"The literal definition of pornography is taken from the ancient Greek porne, meaning female sexual slaves, and graphos, meaning writings or graphic depictions thereof" [8] As time has went by there have been many depictions of pornography, but the real quarrel started in the 1600's. "Danish criminologist Berl Kutchinsky traces the beginnings of modern pornography to the 1650s, when three pornographic classics appeared." [9]

Today the statistics reveal that pornography has grown into a multi crore industry. As of 2003, there were 1.3 million pornographic websites consisting of 260 million pages[10] Unique worldwide users visiting adult web sites comes to monthly: 72 million.[11] **(Figure1)**

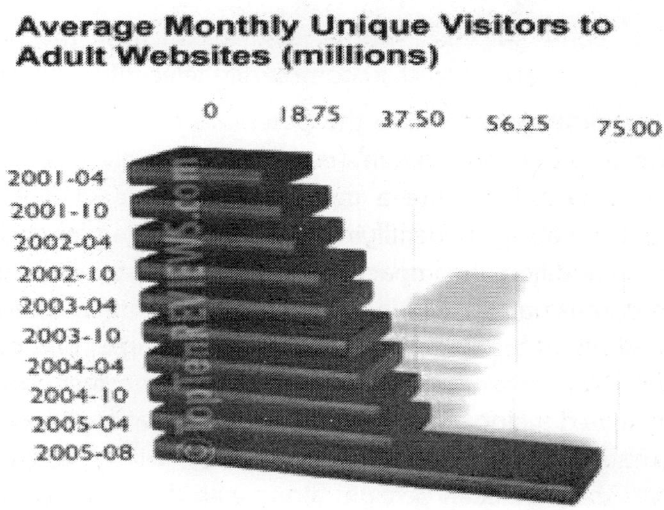

Fig. 1

***Source:* Internet Filter Review**

Data further suggests that every second, there are approximately 28,258 Internet users viewing pornography[12]Approximately one in four Internet search engine requests is related to pornography[13] Every day there are approximately 116,000 online searches for child pornography The total porn industry revenue for 2006 is $97 billion worldwide.[14] With China and Japan sharing the top positions (Figure2).

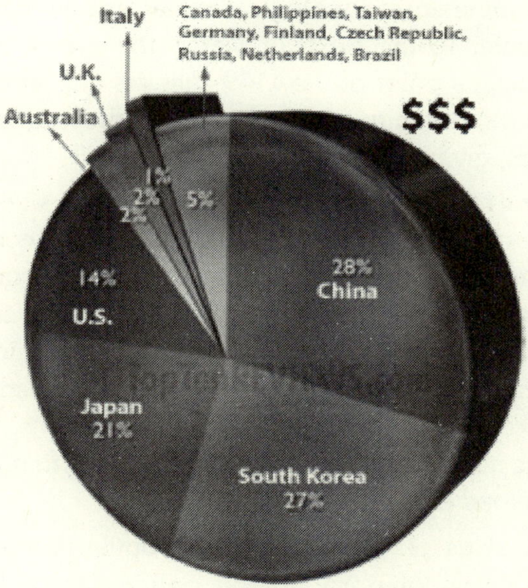

Fig. 2. Visiters Division by Country.

***Source :* Internet Filter Review**

The pornography industry is larger than the revenues of the top technology companies combined: Microsoft, Google, Amazon, eBay, Yahoo!, Apple, Netflix and EarthLink.[15] As a result of the huge market on the web for pornography and the competition among sites, the pornographic images have become rougher, more violent, and degrading.[16]

The rapid growth of Internet usage has been identified as the primary reason for the exponential increase in pornography use and production, as well as compulsive sexual behaviors related to pornography use.[17] Some of the new technologies which aids this process consists of

- **Digital Video Disk (DVD)**, which provides high quality videos and interactive capabilities for the viewer. While making the videos, scenes can be shot from multiple angles, and all points of view can be added to a CD ROM. The viewer can then choose the version, point of view, or camera angle he/she prefers. Viewers can watch the movie in chronological order, moving from one character to the next, or watch the movie from one character's point of view. 49 Viewers can interact with DVD movies in much the same way they do with video games, giving them a more active role.[18]
- **Usenet newsgroups** are still popular sites for the exchange of information on how to find women and children for sexual exploitation.[19] Although much media attention is given to child pornography rings and cases that use sophisticated technologies to keep their activities secret, such as the W0nderland Club that used a Soviet KGB code to encrypt all its communications, the older public newsgroups are still commonly used to upload and download child pornography.[20]
- **Web sites** are the other most popular venue for the distribution of pornography online. Large legal sex industry businesses have sophisticated web sites with subscription fees that bring in millions of dollars per year.[21] There are also tens of thousands of free pornography sites that are maintained by amateurs or someone making a relatively small amount of money from advertising banners for larger sites and businesses.[22]

The Internet has made sexual exploitation of and violence against women and children seem more normal, and this is a matter of deep concern. Criminal syndicates violate laws prohibiting sexual exploitation and violence by locating their servers in host countries with less restrictive laws, to avoid regulation. The new technologies have thus enabled the creation of online communities free from interference or standards where any and every type of sexual violence goes and where women-hating is the norm.[23] Over the past ten years, the Internet has emerged as the premier forum of the international sex trade and has facilitated, accelerated, and normalised the sexual exploitation of women and girls New ICTs have combined with racism, sexism, and capitalism to escalate sexual exploitation worldwide.[24]

Regarding the impact of the Internet on sexuality generally, Greenfield [25] assert, Since its inception, the Internet has been associated with sexuality in a kind of synergistic dance, each fueling the transformation of the other. The influence of the Internet on sexuality is likely to be so significant that it will ultimately be recognized as the cause of the next "sexual revolution".[26] This synergistic dance, however, has caused others to argue that pornography and on-line sexual pursuits are "... a hidden public health hazard exploding, in part because very few are recognizing it as such or taking it seriously"[27]

Though there are differing views on the effects of Pornography, generally it is found to be not only destructive to people in general, but degrading to women as well. Pornography is degrading to women because it serves as an instruction manual for violent sexual acts, it portrays violence against women as an acceptable thing, and it portrays women as useless sex toys. Therefore, the explicit content of pornography is degrading in many ways to the women of our country.[28] But there are others who point out that generally it was believed that men were the sole consumers of pornography while adult women were the primary staple of pornographic images. The Internet era, however, has fostered a level-playing field of sorts and more and more women are producing, viewing and interacting with the sex industry than ever before.

Some greet this cultural shift enthusiastically, claiming that it helps women own and express their sexuality[29]Although men are 6.43 times more likely to use Internet pornography than females[30] women represent 30 percent of Internet pornography consumers[31] Some women describe their experiences with pornography as positive. The Feminist Anti-Censorship Taskforce (FACT), for example, filed a brief against the Indianapolis City Council in Hudnut,[32] claiming that pornography may be a source of liberation and pleasure.[33] They pointed out that Indeed, pornography brings benefits to women. In censoring pornography, the state will impoverish rather than enrich them. Lisa Duggan explains:

> "The existence of pornography has served to flout conventional sexual mores, to ridicule sexual hypocrisy and to underscore the importance of sexual needs. Pornography carries many messages . . . it advocates sexual adventure, sex outside of marriage, sex for pleasure, casual sex, illegal sex, anonymous sex, public sex, voyeuristic sex. Some of these ideas appeal to women reading or seeing pornography, who may interpret some images as legitimating their own sense of sexual urgency or desire to be sexually aggressive."[34]

Although pornography may be pleasing to some women, it may terrorize others. For example, Andrea Dworkin describes a female response to a pornographic photograph of a woman, spread eagle, bound by ropes to the top of a Jeep in Hustler magazine: "The terror is implicit in the content of the photograph, but beyond that the photograph strikes the female viewer dumb with fear. One perceives that the bound woman must be in pain. The very power to make the photograph (to use the model, to tie her in that way) and the fact of the photograph (the fact that someone did use the model, did tie her in that way, that the photograph is published in a magazine and seen by millions of men who buy it specifically to see such photographs) evoke fear in the female observer unless she entirely dissociates herself from the photograph: refuses to believe or understand that real persons posed for it, refuses to see the bound person as a woman like herself. Terror is finally the content of the photograph, and it is also its effect on the female observer.[35]

Many consider pornography as gender violence that violates the civil rights of women. Anti-porn activist Catherine MacKinnon once explained, "We are proposing a statutory scheme that will situate pornography as a central practice in the subordination of women.[36] But why is pornography viewed as violence in the first place, and not merely words or images? This view was well embodied in the much-cited Minneapolis anti-porn ordinance of 1983.[37] The ordinance stated that all women who worked in porn were coerced, and could bring a civil lawsuit against producers and distributors. Coercion was deemed to be present even if the woman was of age, she fully understood the nature of the performance.[38] The relationship between particularly sexually violent images in the media and subsequent aggression...is much stronger statistically than the relationship between smoking and lung cancer." Edward Donnerstein, Larry Baron and Murray Straus undertook a 50-state correlational analysis of reported rape rates and the circulation rates of eight pornographic magazines: *Chic, Club, Forum, Gallery, Genesis, Hustler, Oui*, and *Playboy*. [39]A highly significant correlation (+0.64) was found between reported rape rates and circulation rates. Baron and Straus attempted to ascertain what other factors might possibly explain this correlation. Their statistical analysis revealed that the proliferation of pornographic magazines and the level of urbanization explained more of the variance in rape rates than the other variables investigated for example, social disorganization, economic inequality, unemployment, sexual inequality.[40]

"Pornography is the theory; rape is the practice," wrote feminist author Robin Morgan.[41] In 1986, a US federal commission concurred. Some kinds of pornography, it concluded, are bound to lead to "increased sexual violence." Indianapolis passed a law allowing women to sue producers for sexual assaults caused by material depicting women in "positions of servility or submission or display. "The campaign fizzled when the courts said the ordinance was an unconstitutional form of "thought control."[42]

In its landmark ruling in *Butler* v. *Her Majesty the Queen*, [43] the Supreme Court of Canada upheld the constitutionality of Canada's obscenity statute, which criminalizes the publication and distribution of obscene materials, defined as those that have as a "dominant characteristic" the "undue exploitation of sex."[44] Moreover, the Canadian Supreme Court expressly recognized that pornography not only affects men and men's behavior, but also corrodes women's integrity and self-esteem. The Court wrote: "if true equality between male and female persons is to be achieved, we cannot ignore the threat to equality resulting from exposure to audiences of certain types of violent and degrading material. Materials portraying women as a class as objects for sexual exploitation and abuse have a negative impact on "the individual's sense of self-worth and acceptance."[45]

But if we analyse the US Supreme Court has not applied similar insight to the pornography of women. But some of the judgments do point out tat pornography directly harms women. In *American Booksellers Association, Inc.* v. *Hudnut*, court, explained:

Depictions of subordination tend to perpetuate subordination. The subordinate status of women in turn leads to affront and lower pay at work, insult and injury at home, battery and rape on the streets. In the language of the legislature, "[p]ornography is central in creating and maintaining sex as a basis of discrimination. Pornography is a systematic practice of exploitation and subordination based on sex which differentially harms women. The bigotry and contempt it produces, with the acts of aggression it fosters, harm women's opportunities for equality and rights [of all kinds]."[4647]

Pornography may well impact upon behavior, although recent studies question the extent. But it is extraordinarily difficult objectively to measure that impact. Various studies document the negative effect of pornography Diana Russell, pornography "predisposes some males to desire rape or intensifies this desire."[48] She further notes in her book Rape and Marriage the correlation between deviant behavior including abuse and pornography. She also found that pornography leads men and women to experience conflict, suffering, and sexual dissatisfaction.[49] Psychologist Edward Donnerstein found that brief exposure to violent forms of pornography can lead to anti-social attitudes and behavior. Male viewers tend to be more aggressive towards women, less responsive to pain and suffering of rape victims, and more willing to accept various myths about rape.[50]Dr. Dolf Zimmerman and Dr. Jennings Bryant showed that continued exposure to pornography had serious adverse effects on beliefs about sexuality in general and on attitudes toward women in particular. They also found that pornography desensitizes people to rape as a criminal offense.[51] These researchers also found that massive exposure to pornography encourages a desire for increasingly deviant materials which involve violence, like sadomasochism and rape.[52]

Many others have also agreed in the point that because the violent acts committed in pornography seem to be acceptable, it may seem to some that these acts are acceptable in everyday life. If a man watching pornography sees a woman being forced to perform oral sex at gunpoint, he may perceive this as an acceptable act and proceed to commit this act of violence himself. The same is also true for younger males who are still in the experimental stages of sexual acts.[53]

A number of studies and surveys have shown that one of the initial impacts pornography has on a developing, adolescent mind is that it evokes upset and distress when one is not psychologically able to process the images.[54] Youth ages 11 to 17 in an Australian survey,[55] used the words "sick," "yuck," "disgusted," "repulsed," and "upset" to describe how they felt about exposure to online sexual material. If the upset or distress was a fleeting occurrence, it may not be as concerning; however, we know that early exposures to pornography leave a lasting and mostly negative impression,[56] and that females report more negative memories of sexually explicit content than males.[57]

International

In USA the world leader of pornography, the legal status of Internet pornography is still somewhat unsettled. In 1968 one of the Supreme Court decision which held that people could view whatever they wished in the privacy of their own homes caused Congress to fund and appoint a commission to study pornography. The commission's report recommended sex education, funding of research into the effects of pornography, restriction of children's access to pornography, and recommended against any restrictions for adults. The report was widely criticized and rejected by Congress. [58] The legality of pornography has been traditionally determined by the Miller test [59] The Miller test was developed in the 1973 case *Miller v. California*. It was laid down

- Whether the average person, applying contemporary community standards, would find that the work, taken as a whole, appeals to the prurient interest,
- Whether the work depicts/describes, in a patently offensive way, sexual conduct or excretory functions specifically defined by applicable state law,
- Whether the work, taken as a whole, lacks serious literary, artistic, political or scientific value. (This is also known as the *SLAPS test*- Serious, Literary, Artistic, Political, and Scientific.) The work is considered obscene only if all three conditions are satisfied.[60]

In 1985, another commission was appointed to study pornography issues, specifically to overturn the findings of the Lockhart commission. It was headed known as the *Meese commission*. The commission's report, released in 1986, found that pornography is harmful and can lead to violent acts. [61]The first real attempt to regulate pornography on the Internet was the federal Communications Decency Act of 1996, which prohibited the "knowing" transmission of "indecent" messages to minors and the publication of materials which depict, in a manner "patently offensive as measured by contemporary community standards, sexual or excretory activities or organs", unless those materials were protected from access by minors.[62] But it quickly fell to a legal challenge brought by the American Civil Liberties Union (ACLU) and a coalition of major publishers. Bringing a traditional First Amendment case against censorship, they argued successfully that the law was too broad 1996, the Supreme Court by 7-2 vote in *American Civil Liberties Union v. Reno*[63] held that the law unconstitutionally abridged freedom of Speech and thus struck down key provisions. Seeking to update federal child pornography law for the Internet, Congress passed the Child Pornography Prevention Act (CPPA) of 1996.[64] Among other features, the law criminalized any visual depiction that "appears to be" child pornography, including so-called virtual porn created by computer. After lower courts struck down provisions of the statute, the U.S. Supreme Court agreed to hear an appeal in *Ashcroft v. Free Speech Coalition*[65], struck down two overbroad provisions of the Child Pornography Prevention Act of 1996 because they abridged "the freedom to engage in a substantial amount of lawful speech. In Jan 21, 2009. The US Supreme Court ruled that a federal law designed to keep Internet pornography away from children violated constitutional free-speech rights. The high court rejected a Justice Department appeal defending the law and handed a victory to those who argued that the efforts of Congress to regulate cyberspace by keeping minors away from online pornography infringed on free-speech rights. The law in question required that website operators use credit cards or adult access codes and personal identification numbers to keep minors from seeing harmful pornography. Violators faced up to six months in prison and fines of as much as $50,000 a day.[66] Another attempt at regulating pornography was in the form of code 2252 that deals with misleading domain names on the Internet which read

(a) Whoever knowingly uses a misleading domain name on the Internet with the intent to deceive a person into viewing material constituting obscenity shall be fined under this title or imprisoned not more than 2 years, or both.

(b) Whoever knowingly uses a misleading domain name on the Internet with the intent to deceive a minor into viewing material that is harmful to minors on the Internet shall be fined under this title or imprisoned not more than 10 years, or both.

The term "material that is harmful to minors" means any communication, consisting of nudity, sex, or excretion, that, taken as a whole and with reference to its context—

(1) predominantly appeals to a prurient interest of minors;

(2) is patently offensive to prevailing standards in the adult community as a whole with respect to what is suitable material for minors; and

(3) lacks serious literary, artistic, political, or scientific value for minors.[67]

In England and Wales, the main legislation on pornographic materials is the Obscene Publications Act 1959, [68] the Obscene Publications Act 1964, and the Indecent Displays Control Act 1981 [69]and Sections 63 to 68 of the Criminal Justice and Immigration Act 2008 .[70] Sweden has no age laws for the possession or viewing of pornography. Some shops follow a voluntary limit and do not sell to minors. It is illegal for persons below the age of 18 to act in porn films or pose for obscene photography. Videos and pictures are illegal if they feature persons under 18, even if the material was legal in the originating country.[71]

Denmark is the first country in the world to legalize pornography. People in Denmark have free access to pornography; Pornography material is legal in Canada to anyone over the age of majority 18 or 19, depending on the province. Sales to persons under 18 (or 19) are prohibited, though persons of this age may own or possess porn.[72] Pornography is legal in Romania also. But some of the prominent countries which has banned pornography includes Saudia Arabia, Iran, Syria, Bahrain, Egypt, UAE, Kuwait, Malaysia, Indonesia, Singapore, Kenya, India, Cuba, China and Brazil.

At the international level Art 6 of Convention on the Elimination of al1 Forms of Discrimination Against Women (CEDAW convention urges States Parties to take all appropriate measures, including legislation, to suppress all forms of traffic in women and exploitation of prostitution of women.[73] Beiging Declaration of women also highlighted the issue of technology and women. Declaration pointed out that the continued projection of negative and degrading images of women in media communications - electronic, print, visual and audio - must be changed. Print and electronic media in most countries do not provide a balanced picture of women's diverse lives and contributions to society in a changing world. In addition, violent and degrading or pornographic media products are also negatively affecting women and their participation in society.[74] Women should be empowered by enhancing their skills, knowledge and access to information technology. This will strengthen their ability to combat negative portrayals of women internationally and to challenge instances of abuse of the power of an increasingly important industry.

The effects of pornography and the need to regulate it

internationally gained prominence in 1990s. General Assembly adopted a resolution on the need to adopt efficient international measures for the prevention and eradication of the sale of children, child prostitution and child pornography Resolution expressed deep concern at the alarming increase in violations of the rights of the child worldwide, in particular the growing number of incidents related to the sale of children, child prostitution and child pornography; It urged the Urges Governments to continue searching for solutions, as well as ways and means of enhancing international cooperation to eradicate such aberrant practices. Further the resolution expressed its support for the work of the Special Rapporteur appointed by the Commission on Human Rights to examine all over the world the question of the sale of children, child prostitution and child pornography, and urges him to continue his efforts in the discharge of his mandate.[75]

Following the resolution Economic and Social Security Council has urged the countries to take effective measures,

- to the extent consistent with freedom of expression, to combat the growing sexualization and use of pornography in media content,
- in terms of the rapid development of ICT, encourage the media to refrain from presenting women as inferior beings and exploiting them as sexual objects and commodities,
- combat ICT- and mediabased violence against women including criminal misuse of ICT for sexual harassment, sexual exploitation and trafficking in women and girls, and support the development and use of ICT as a resource for the empowerment of women and girls, including those affected by violence, abuse and other forms of sexual exploitation;[76]

Another note worthy initiative aimed at controlling pornography is the draft Declaration of Principles by World

Summit on Information Society(WSIS) It urges all actors in the Information Society should seek to promote the common good, protect privacy, and to prevent abusive uses of ICTs, such as criminal conduct based on acts of racial discrimination, xenophobia, pornography/obscenity and paedophilia. The freedom of use of ICTs should respect human rights and fundamental freedoms of others, including personal privacy, These values are particularly relevant when commercial activities are conducted through networks.[77] It can be easily gauged that pornography many times violates the dignity and privacy of women.

An analysis of these legislative initiative suggests that most of the regulations and restrictions was against Child Pornography .Regarding the exploitation of women most of the legislative initiatives were silent. This lacuna is more prominent in relation to new age ICT aided pornography where national legislations are normally weak and does not have much of force in the wake of these new technologies.

Indian Legislative and Judicial Framework

The term 'pornography' when used in relation to an offence is not defined in any statutes in India but the term 'obscenity' has been effectively explained in two statutes in India, and these legislations prescribe that 'obscenity' in certain circumstances constitutes an offence. These legislations are

- The Indian Penal Code, 1860 ('IPC') and
- The Information Technology Act, 2000 ('IT Act').

Section 292 of the IPC comprehensively sets out the circumstances in which 'obscenity' and / or any 'obscene' material is an offence. According to section 292,

(i) "whoever sells, lets to hire, distributes, publicly exhibits or in any manner puts into circulation, or for purposes of sale, hire, distribution, public exhibition or circulation, makes, produces or has in his possession any obscene book, pamphlet, paper, drawing, painting, representation, or figure or any other obscene object whatsoever or

(ii) imports, exports or conveys any obscene object for any of the purposes mentioned in (i) above, or knowing or having reason to believe that such obscene object will be sole, let to hire, distributed or publicly exhibited or in any manner out into circulation, or

(iii) takes part in or receives profits from any business in the course of which he knows or has reason to believe that any such obscene objects are, for any of the purposes mentioned in (i) above, made, produced, purchased, kept, imported, exported, conveyed, publicly exhibited or in any manner put into circulation, or

(iv) advertises or makes known by any means whatsoever that any person is engaged or is ready to engage in any act which is an offence under section 292 or that any such obscene object can be procured from or through any person or (v) offers or attempts to do any act which is an offence under section 292, is punishable with imprisonment and fine. Therefore, obscenity is an offence if it falls within any of the above prescribed purposes.[78]

Section 292 also sets out the purposes under which obscenity is not deemed to be an offence and these are when any such material is used (i) justifiably for the public good for e.g. interest of science, literature, art or learning or other purposes of general concern (ii) for bona-fide religious purposes and (iii) in any ancient monument within the meaning of the Ancient Monuments and Archeological Sites and Remains Act, 1958 or in any temple, or on any car used for the conveyance of idols.[79]

From a plain reading of Section 292 of the IPC it appears that if a person is in mere possession of the obscene material for his personal use without any intention to perform any of the purposes specified in section 292 it may not be an offence under section 292. In the case of *Jagdish Chavla and others* v. *the State of Rajasthan*, [80] the accused was caught viewing an obscene film on the television with the help of a VCR which along with the cassette was seized and a case under section 292 of the IPC was registered. The accused filed a petition in the High Court for quashing of the proceedings and it was held that simply being in possession of a blue film could not make a person guilty under section 292 unless it was further proved that the purpose of keeping the same was selling or letting it on hire. However, it would be prudent to be aware that a prosecution may lie for mere possession of obscene material also. It could be argued that a person, even though he is in mere possession of the obscene material which may be for his own personal use, actually aids and abets the publication, sale, hire, distribution etc of the obscene material, which is an offence under section 292. And under section 111 of the IPC, the abettor is held to be equally guilty of the offence which he has abetted provided it is proved that the offence is a probable consequence of the abetment. [81]

Obscenity Under the Information Technology Act 2000

Section 67 of the IT Act lays down the law that obscenity is an offence when it is published or transmitted or caused to be published in any electronic form.[82]

The expressions, 'publishing' or 'transmission' have not been specifically defined under the IT Act, but the commentaries suggest that 'publishing means making information available to people'. Transmission may be addressed to an intended recipient for his personal use. But that is not relevant. The act of 'transmission' is sufficient to constitute an offence under section 67 of the IT Act. Therefore if any obscene material is published or transmitted in any electronic form it is an offence under section 67 of the IT Act. The transmission' and not mere possession, of obscene information is an offence The provisions of section 67 of the IT Act are therefore similar to section 292 of the IPC where mere possession of the obscene material for ones own personal use may not be construed as on offence, however, it would be advisable to be cognizant of the fact that the prosecution can take a plea of abetment in a case of mere possession.[83]

In the context of cybercafés in particular, if a customer downloads any obscene material for his personal viewing on the terminal assigned to him and this fact is known to the owner of the cybercafé it would constitute an offence and the owner of the cybercafé would be liable under section 292 of the IPC read with Section 67 of the IT Act. Provided however, if it is established that this act was without the knowledge of the owner of the cybercafé it could be difficult for the prosecution to sustain its plea under section 292 of the IPC and section 67 of the IT Act. The law relating to the liability of cybercafé owners under these provisions of the IPC and the IT Act is not very well settled and therefore open to subjective interpretation. To mitigate liability and to avoid possible criminal prosecution the cybercafé owners could perhaps make an attempt to take protection under section 79 of the IT Act,[84] which absolves 'intermediaries', who only provide access to content but do not provide content itself, by extending the argument of intermediaries to cybercafés (although not tested in courts in India). The grounds of defense could be also made stronger by setting up a mechanism (hardware or software) whereby the customers are prevented from accessing any obscene websites and disclaimers are displayed prominently informing customers that obscenity is an offence which is punishable with imprisonment and that despite the warning, if customers still view such websites, they will be personally responsible and not the owner of the cybercafé.[85]

Under the circumstances, the law as it stands on obscenity with regard to the liability it imposes on the owners of cybercafés is certainly not free from doubt and casts an onerous obligation on them to successfully defend a prosecution under the relevant provisions of the IPC and the IT Act. However, if certain precautions are observed such as establishing mechanisms which block such websites and displaying the disclaimers as suggested above, prominently, at least may help in providing a good defense.

Regarding the punishment if we analyse the sections under section 292 of the IPC for the first conviction a term of imprisonment (simple or rigorous) which may extend to two years, and with fine which may extend to two thousand rupees, and in the event of a second or subsequent convictions, with imprisonment (simple or rigorous) for a term which may extend to five years, and also with fine which may extend to five thousand rupees.[86] The punishment for an offence under section 67 of the IT Act is on first conviction with imprisonment (simple or rigorous) for a term which may extend to five years, and with fine which may extend to one lakh rupees, and in the event of a second or subsequent convictions, with imprisonment (simple or rigorous) for a term which may extend to ten years, and also with fine which may extend to two lakh rupees.[87]

Conclusion

The use of new communication and information technologies for the sexual exploitation of women and children is creating a crisis for women s status, rights, and dignity all over the world. Pimps, traffickers, stalkers, and users of pornography and women and children in prostitution have adopted new technologies to further their abuse and exploitation of women and children.[88] The use of new communications and information technologies in the sexual exploitation of women and children will continue to grow with the increased number of users on the internet. Internationally, there have been governmental and law enforcement responses to distribution of child pornography, However, there is little governmental intervention to stop the sexual exploitation of adult women. The existing mechanisms are clearly inadequate to cater to the imposing challenge. The problem with internet technologies is that they try to avoid the responsibilities by locating their server in those countries where pornography is either legal or where fewer restrictions are provided. It is imperative in the interests of dignity of women that international community comes up with a unique legally binding convention to tackle the exploitation of women.

References

1 Govt. Cracks Censor Whip on Savita Bhabhi available on http://www.merinews.com/catFull.jsp?articleID=15774431 Last visited on 26-06-2009.

2 Govt Bans Popular Toon Porn Site Savitabhabhi.com; Mounting Concern Over Censorship.

3 Savita Bhabhi influences 11-year-old boy to send obscene mail to his teacher available on http://www.alootechie.com/content/savitabhabhi-influences-11-year-old-boy-send-obscene-mail-his-teacher Last visited on 3-07-2009).

4 Praveen Dalal, "Use of ICT for Women Empowerment in India available" on http://unpan1.un.org/intradoc/groups/public/documents/APCITY/UNPAN029838.pdf last visited on 4-06-2009.

5 Gender Equality and Empowerment of Women through ICT, Women 2000and Beyond ,United nations 2005.

6 ICT and Gender Equality, Gender and Development Group, The World Bank, October 2006.

7 Gurumurthy,,e-Choupal, for example, is a much celebrated initiative. Their agriculture extension efforts in India which seek to improve the productivity of agriculturists are based on the telecentre model. e-Choupal has been critiqued for not involving low-caste farmers. Women are also not seen as intended beneficiaries of the initiative.

8 Marianna Beck,The Roots of Western pornography", The Journal Of Sex and Sexuality, p 35, 2000.

9 Berl Kutchinsky "Studies on Pornography and Sex Crimes in Denmark, New Social Science Monographs, Denmark 1970.

10 Internet pornography statistics , Internet filter review available on http://internet-filter-review.toptenreviews.com/internet-pornography-statistics.html last visited on 4-06-2009.

11 Id.

12 Internet Pornography Statistics, 2008.

13 Id.

14 Id.

15 Id.

16 Frank Rich, Naked Capitalists, N.Y. Times Magazine, May 20, p 51 2001.

17 Schneider, J. P. . Effects of Cybersex Addiction on the Family: Results of a survey. Sexual Addiction & Compulsivity, 7, 31-58.,2000 Schneider, J. P. A Qualitative Study of Cybersex Participants: Gender Differences, Recovery Issues, and Implications for Therapists. Sexual Addiction & Compulsivity, 7, 249-278, 2000.

18 Karen Kaplan, Pushing Porn On DVDs, L.A. TIMES, Jan. 9, a 1, 2001.

19 Id.

20 Stuart Miller, Technological Level of Wonderland Network Shocked All Investigators, IRISH TIMES, Sept. 3, 15 ,1998.

21 Donna M. Hughes, "The Internet and Sex Industries: Partners in Global Sexual Exploitation", IEEE Technology & Society Magazine, p 35, (2000).

22 Id.

23 Berkman Center for Internet and Society, 'The Internet and the Sex Industry', see http://cyber.law.harvard.edu/vaw02/. Last visited on 3-07-2009.

24 http://cyber.law.harvard.edu/vaw02/module2.html last visited on 4-07-2009.

25 Greenfield, P. M. In advertent Exposure to Pornography on the Internet: Implications for Peer-to-peer file Sharing Networks for Child Development and families. Applied Developmental Psychology, 25, 741–750,2004.

26 Id.

27 Cooper, A. & Griffin-Shelley, E. A Quick Tour of Online Sexuality: Part 1. American Psychotherapy, November/December, 11-13.,2002. Delmonico, D. L., Griffin, E. J., & Moriarty, J. Cybersex unhooked: A workbook or breaking free from compulsive online sexual behavior. Center City: MN: Hazelden Educational Press, (2001).

28 Id.

29 Jill C. Manning, The Impact of Pornography on Women: Social Science Findings and Clinical Observations, 2008.

30 Stack, S., Wasserman, I., & Kern, R. Adult Social Bonds and Use of Internet Pornography. Social Science Quarterly, 85(1), 75-88,(2004).

31 Supra note 12 See Internet Pornography Statistics 2008.

32 American Booksellers Ass'n v. Hudnut, 771 F.2d 323, 332 (7th Cir. 1985), aff'd without opinion, 475 U.S. 1001 (1986).

33 Nan D. Hunter & Sylvia A. Law, Brief Amici Curiae of Feminist Anti-Censorship Taskforce, et al., in American Booksellers Association v. Hudnut, 21 U. MICH. J.L. REF. 69, 74 (1987-1988).

34 Wendy McElroy, Banning Pornography Endangers Women, available on http://www.isil.org/resources/lit/banning-porn.html last visited on 3-06-2009.

35 Andrea Dworkin, Pornography : Men Possessing Women at xxx-xxxi (1989).

36 MacKinnon, Catharine A., Toward a Feminist Theory of the State. Cambridge, MA: Harvard University Press,(1989).

37 Sporre, Stuart. Compilation of Material Relating to the Minneapolis Pornography Ordinannce, 1984.

38 Supra note 34 See Wendy.

39 Donnerstein, Edward. Unpublished transcript of testimony to the Public Hearings on Ordinances to Add Pornography as Discrimination against Women. Committee on Government Operations, City Council, Minneapolis, MN pp. 4-12, 1983.

40 Diana Russel, Pornography: The Evidence of Har, (Berkeley, California: Russell Publications, 1994).

41 Robin Mrogan, "Theory and Practice: Pornography and Rape", in Going Too Far: The Personal Chronicle of a Feminist, 1974.

42 Steve Chapman, Is Pornography a Catalyst of sexual violence, available on http://www.reason.com/news/show/123330.html last visited on 4-06-2009.

43 [1992] 1 S.C.R. 452 (1992) (Can.).

44 Criminal Code, R.S.C. ch. C-46, 163(8) (1985) (Can.) ("For the purposes of this Act, any publication a dominant characteristic of which is the undue exploitation of sex, or of sex and any one or more of the following subjects, namely, crime, horror, cruelty and violence, shall be deemed to be obscene").

45 Butler, [1992] 1 S.C.R. at 479.

46 771 F.2d 323 (7th Cir. 1985), aff'd without opinion, 475 U.S. 1001, 1986.

47 Rebecca L. Eisenberg, Pornography, Equality, and a Disrimination-Free

Workplace: A Comparitive Perspective, 106 Harvard Law Review 1075, 1993.

48 Diana Russel, Against Pornography: The Evidence of Harm, Berkeley, Calif., 1993.

49 Diana Russlel, Bloomington: Indiana University Press, 1990.

50 Edward Donnerstein, Pornography and Violence Against Women, 1980.

51 Pornography, Sexual Callousness, and the Trivialization of Rape," Journal of Communication, 1982.

52 The Effect of Erotica Featuring Sadomasochism and Bestiality of Motivated Inter-Male Aggressions," Personality and Social Psychology Bulletin, 1981.

53 http://www.oppapers.com/essays/Pornography-Degrading-Women/57556 Last accessed on 23-07-2009.

54 Mitchell, K. J., Finkelhor, D., & Wolak, J. The exposure of youth to unwanted sexual material on the Internet: A national survey of risk, impact, and prevention. Youth & Society, 34(3), 330–358, 2003.

55 Flood, M., & Hamilton, C. Youth and pornography in Australia: Evidence on the extent of exposure and likely effects. The Australia Institute, Discussion Paper Number 52, 1322-5421, 2003.

56 Cantor, J., Mares, M. L., & Hyde, J. S., Autobiographical memories of exposure to sexual media content. Media Psychology, 5, 1–31,2003. In Greenfield, P. M. , Inadvertent exposure to pornography on the Internet: Implications for peer-to-peer file sharing networks for child development and families. Applied Developmental Psychology, 25, 741–750, (2004).

57 Id.

58 Lockart report concluded that there was no evidence demonstrating any significant social harm from pornography depicting consenting adults, and recommended that existing obscenity laws should be repealed. President Nixon refused to accept either the report or the commission's conclusions.

59 413 U.S. 15 (1973.

60 Id.

61 Pat Califia,, The Obscene, Disgusting, and Vile Meese Commission Report,1986. Report wanted stepping up enforcement of existing obscenity laws; increased cooperation between local, state, and federal law enforcement personnel and the IRS; and a computerized national database. They want forfeiture statutes, so that any proceeds from production of pornography can be confiscated.

62 Communications Decency Act ,The CDA imposed broadcast-style content regulations on the open, decentralized Internet and severely restricted the first amendment rights of all Americans. CDT strongly opposed this legislation because it threatened the very existence of the Internet as a means for free expression, education, and political discourse. Although well intentioned, the CDA was ineffective and failed to recognize the unique nature of this global, decentralized medium.

63 521 U.S. 844 (1997).

64 Child Pornography Prevention Act is a United States federal law to restrict child pornography on the internet, including virtual child pornography. The Child Pornography Prevention Act added two categories of speech to the definition of child pornography. The first prohibited "any visual depiction, including any photograph, film, video, picture, or computer or computer-generated image or picture" that "is, or appears to be, of a minor engaging in sexually explicit conduct.

65 535 U.S. 234 (2002).

66 US court brands pornography law unconstitutional, The Dawn , Jan, 22, 2009.

67 18 USC 2252 - Sec. 2252B. Misleading domain names on the Internet.

68 Obscene Publications Act 1959, law relating to the publication of obscene matter; to provide for the protection of literature; and to strengthen the law concerning pornography.

69 Indecent Displays Control Act 1981,It is concerned with preventing the display of "indecent" material to the unsuspecting public.

70 Criminal Justice and Immigration Act 2008.

71 http://news.bbc.co.uk/2/hi/europe/655251.stm last visited on 3006-2009.

72 Nick Gier, A Denmark Retrospective : Fond Memories For Me and 41 years of Socioeconomic Progress for the days available on http://www.newwest.net/main/article/a_denmark_retrospective_fond_memories_for_me/Last visited on 3-07-2009.

73 UN GA Res 34/180, UN Doc A/34/46, 19 I.L.M. 33 (1980).

74 Platform For Action, Beijing Conference 1995.

75 A/RES/49/210, 1995.

76 Participation and access of women to the media, and information and communications technologies and their impact on and us e as an instrument for the advancement and empowerment of women United Nations-Economic and Social Council /Division for the Advancement of Women, Document WSIS/PC-3/CONTR/22-E, 2003.

77 Our Common Vision of the Information SocietyOur Common Vision of the Information Society, Draft Declaration of Principles, Document WSIS/PC-3/DT/1(Rev.2 B)-E.

78 Indian penal Code Section 292.

79 Id.

80 1999 CR LJ 2562.

81 Lekhesh Dholakia, Opinion The law on Pornography in India and implication on cyber café operators, available on http://www.apiap.org/opinions/legal/opinion-the-law-on-pornography-in-india-and-implication-on-cyber-cafe-operators last visited on 5-07-2009.

82 Section 67 Information Technology Act 2000 Whoever publishes or transmits or causes to be published in the electronic form, any material which is lascivious or appeals to the prurient interest or if its effect is such as to tend to deprave and corrupt persons who are likely, having regard to all relevant circumstances, to read, see or hear the matter contained or embodied in it, shall be punished on first conviction with imprisonment of either description for a term which may extend to five years and with fine which may extend to one lakh rupees and in the event of a second or subsequent conviction with imprisonment of either description for a term which may extend to ten years and also with fine which may extend to two lakh rupees.

83 Supra note 81.

84 Id.

85 Id.

86 Supra note 78 Section 292 Indian Penal Code.

87 Supra note 82 Section 67, Information Technology Act 2000.

88 Donna M. Hughes, The Use of New Communications and Information Technologies for Sexual Exploitation of Women and Children, Hastings Women's Law Journal, Vol. 13:1 129-130, 2001.